Dash Diet Air Fryer Beginners 2022

1000 Days of Quick & Easy Low Sodium Recipes for a Heart-Healthy Lifestyle | 35 Days Flexible Meal Plan Included

Table of Contents

Introduction 5
    What Is The DASH Diet? 5
    A Quick History of the DASH Diet 5
    Dietary Recommendations for DASH Diet 5
        Grains: 6-8 Servings per Day 6
        Vegetables: 4-5 Servings per Day 6
        Fruits: 4-5 Servings per Day 6
        Dairy: 2-3 Servings per Day 6
        Nuts and Seeds: 4-5 Servings per Week 6
        Fats: 2-3 Servings per Day 6
        Sweets: 5 Servings or Fewer per Week 6
    Sodium Recommendations 6
    What To Eat 7
    What Not To Eat 7
    Benefits of the DASH Diet 7
    Lowering Your Blood Pressure 8
        Balance Diet 8
        Less Sodium Intake 8
        Reduce Fat Intake 9
        Exercise 9
        Sleep Well 9
        Don't Smoke 9
        Destress 9

Chapter 1: Breakfast Recipes 10
1. Egg Frittata 11
2. Ezekiel Bread Toast 12
3. Blueberry Yogurt Pancakes 13
4. Buckwheat Crepes 14
5. Blueberry Spelt Muffins 15
6. Breakfast Cookies 16
7. Morning Oats 17
8. Spinach Omelet 18
9. Breakfast Quiches 19
10. Crusted French Toast 20

Chapter 2: Snacks Recipes 22
11. Crispy Beans 23
12. Onion Rings 24
13. Hummus 25
14. Sweet Potato Crisp 26
15. Cardamom Tea Cookies 27
16. Whole-Wheat Pretzel 28
17. Mini-Meatballs 30
18. Potato Pancakes 31
19. Spiced Pita Chips 32

20. Zucchini Chips 33

Chapter 3: Salads Recipes 34

21. Black Bean Salad 35
22. Green Salad With Chickpeas 36
23. Spinach Salad With Maple Dressing.....37
24. Broccoli Salad 38
25. Radish Couscous Salad......................39
26. Brussels Sprout Salad.........................40
27. Spinach Salad With Roasted Sweet Potatoes 41
28. Mushroom Salad 42
29. Napa Cabbage Salad 43
30. Bean Avocado Salad 44

Chapter 4: Soups Recipes...........................45

31. Spicy Sweet Potato Soup 46
32. Barley Carrot Soup............................47
33. Cream Of Mushroom Soup 48
34. Carrot Ginger Soup 49
35. Sweet Potato Lentil Soup....................50
36. Cauliflower Soup................................51
37. Butternut Squash Soup.......................53
38. Lentil Chicken Soup 54
39. French Onion Soup 55

40. Turkey Noodle Soup 56

Chapter 5: Poultry Recipes...........................58

41. Chicken Zucchini Skewers....................59
42. Saucy Duck Breast 60
43. Chicken Wraps..................................61
44. Roasted Chicken 62
45. Chicken Brats....................................63
46. Balsamic Chicken Roast 64
47. Chicken Piccata.................................65
48. Chicken Mushroom Ragu....................66
49. Chicken Quesadillas............................68
50. Crusted Chicken.................................69
51. Honey Dijon Chicken 70
52. Garlic Herb Chicken 71
53. Onion Stuffed Whole Chicken 72
54. Crispy Air fried Chicken 73
55. Sesame Chicken..................................74

Chapter 6: Meat Recipes............................75

56. Spicy Beef Kebabs..............................76
57. Pork Tenderloin With Balsamic Sauce .77
58. Pork With Herbes De Provence 78
59. Pork Chops With Black Currant Sauce .79
60. Pork Fajitas.......................................80

#	Recipe	Page
61.	Spiced Pork Medallions	81
62.	Curried Pork Tenderloin	82
63.	Beef Stew With Fennel	83
64.	Beef Brisket Stew	84
65.	Beef Barley Stew	85
66.	Beef Vegetable Kebabs	86
67.	Asian Pork Tenderloin	87
68.	New York Strip Steak	88
69.	Shepherd's Pie	89
70.	Pork Tenderloin With Fennel Sauce	90

Chapter 7: Fish and Seafood Recipes 92

#	Recipe	Page
71.	Chipotle Spiced Shrimp	93
72.	Air fried Cod Pocket	94
73.	Halibut With Tomato Relish	95
74.	Crusted Snapper Curry	96
75.	Grouper With Tomato Sauce	97
76.	Grilled Salmon With Maple Glaze	98
77.	Roasted Salmon	99
78.	Shrimp Kebabs	100
79.	Air Fried Sole	101
80.	Air Fried Swordfish	102

Chapter 8: Vegetarian Recipes 103

#	Recipe	Page
81.	Marinated Mushrooms	104
82.	Barley Risotto	105
83.	Black Bean Wrap	106
84.	Vegetable Kebabs	107
85.	Buffalo Cauliflower	108
86.	Sumac Roasted Cauliflower	109
87.	Sesame-Crusted Tofu	110
88.	Stuffed Eggplant	111
89.	Vegetable Calzone	112
90.	Vegetarian Chilli With Tofu	113

Chapter 9: Desserts Recipes 114

#	Recipe	Page
91.	Tahini Cookies	115
92.	Berry Hand Pies	116
93.	Black Bean Brownie	117
94.	Apple Pie Roll	118
95.	Almond Rice Pudding	119
96.	Apple Hand Pies	120
97.	Air Fryer Beignets	121
98.	Churros	122
99.	Chocolate Souffle	123
100.	Oatmeal Cookies	124

Chapter 10: 35 Day Meal Plan 126

Conclusion 129

Introduction

The road to healthier living is full of challenges and struggles, but it is not impossible to attain better heart health and achieve weight loss. You only need a practical approach, the right direction, and a complete understanding of your body's nutritional needs, and you can crack the code to a healthy lifestyle!

The harms of fad diets are known to all; there is never a quick fix for human health. Our body needs a slow, reliable, and practical dietary approach that could support and improve its everyday metabolism. Dietary approaches to stop hypertension or DASH were created keeping the same in mind. The word "approaches" strongly resonates with what this diet offers – multiple dietary and lifestyle changes to treat hypertension and improve health.

As a fitness consultant and a registered dietician, I have extensively studied the DASH diet and its various health benefits. The recipes in this cookbook result from my personal transition to this new lifestyle. I hope that these 90+ low-sodium nutritious recipes and the dietary guidelines from this cookbook will help you go through your DASH journey easily.

What Is The DASH Diet?

Dietary Approaches to Stop Hypertension or DASH diet is not even a diet- it is a dietary approach that anyone can follow to save themselves from the harmful results of a high sodium intake. People mainly suffering from hypertension or heart diseases can use this diet to keep their blood pressure in control.

According to the statistics given by the Center of Science For Public Interest-CSPI, an average American consumes 3500 mg of sodium in a day, which is responsible for causing high blood pressure and other related health problems. The DASH diet focuses on lower sodium intake and minimal consumption of processed food. It recommends a nutrient-dense diet that must have a lower amount of saturated fat and low caloric content but consume a high amount of proteins, healthy carbs, fibers, and vitamins. As per the DASH diet recommendations, all can be achieved by relying more on lean meat, poultry, seafood, whole grains, legumes, vegetables, fruits, seeds, low-fat or zero fat dairy and nuts, etc., and cutting down consumption of processed food.

A Quick History of the DASH Diet

The studies to treat or prevent hypertension through dietary changes had been going on even before the DASH diet, but the first formal step towards the understanding and effects of the DASH diet was taken in the 1990s. The National Institute of Health NIH in 1992 started funding several medical studies to discover if any dietary intervention would help treat or counter hypertension. The participants of those researches were made to follow just the recommended dietary changes and no other medication. The researchers concluded that only low-sodium and low fat intake for 1-3 months could decrease the subjects' systolic and diastolic blood pressure by 6 to 11 mm Hg on average. Keeping that into account, researchers further worked on the concept, and, later, NIH released a set of guidelines to counter hypertension which was formally named The DASH Diet.

Dietary Recommendations for DASH Diet

Though the DASH diet primarily focuses on slashing sodium from the everyday diet, it also focuses on portion control and low-caloric intake. Portion control is essential for weight loss which is imperative to keeping blood pressure controlled. According to the NIH, a person should consume food as per the following serving sizes:

Grains: 6-8 Servings per Day

Grains are among the most consumed food groups, including rice, pasta, cereal, quinoa, bread, etc. Grains are a good source of complex carbs, fibers, some protein, minerals, and a few vitamins. Because of these benefits and the wide-ranging uses of grains in our diet, they are recommended for 6-8 servings per day. A single serving of grain means one slice of bread, one ounce of cereal, or half a cup of rice or pasta. Now multiply this serving size by 6 or 8 and divide the total amount into three-four meals of the day.

Vegetables: 4-5 Servings per Day

One cup of leafy vegetables and half a cup of other vegetables make one DASH diet serving. So, you can have two cups of vegetables and two cups of leafy greens per day on a dash diet. You can add these vegetables to the salads, pasta, and other savory delights.

Fruits: 4-5 Servings per Day

Half a cup of frozen or canned fruits and one cup of fresh fruit makes a single serving on a DASH diet. Since fruits are a major source of minerals, fibers, and vitamins, they must be consumed in 4-5 servings per day. Fruits are low on sodium and rich in fibers, so it is always healthy to consume them on the DASH diet.

Dairy: 2-3 Servings per Day

A single serving of dairy products on the DASH diet means one cup of low-fat yogurt, skimmed milk, or one and a half-ounce of part-skim cheese. So, you can consume 2-3 such servings in a day.

Nuts and Seeds: 4-5 Servings per Week

Legumes make a food group rich in carbs and plant-sourced proteins, including beans, lentils, split peas, etc. The legumes are paired with nuts and seeds to form one group, consumed in 4-5 servings per day on the DASH diet serving size formula.

Fats: 2-3 Servings per Day

Fats and oils contain three times the calories and energy than carbs; therefore, they must be consumed in a smaller amount in a day. For the Dash diet, 2-3 servings of fats and oil in any form is enough to meet the basic body needs. Try to add healthy unsaturated plant-based fats and oils to the diet to avoid bad cholesterols.

Sweets: 5 Servings or Fewer per Week

Sweets come last on this list, and they must be consumed in a very small amount on the dash diet. Five or fewer servings a week is enough to have on this diet. A single serving of sweet means half a cup of sorbet, one tablespoon of sugar, or one cup of sweet lemonade. So, you can have that single serving on alternate days of the week.

Sodium Recommendations

The goal is to reduce sodium intake to the point where it would stop interfering with the body's blood pressure levels. To achieve that, the DASH diet has two general recommendations:

- Standard: 2500mg or less of sodium per day.
- Low-Intake: 1500mg or less of sodium per day

Someone who is not suffering from hypertension can go with the 2500mg/day standard, while people with high blood pressure must consume 1500mg or less sodium in a day.

What To Eat

Remember the health goals and the aimed benefits of the DASH diet! You need to make healthier dietary choices and consume rich fiber, minerals, proteins, good cholesterol fats, and some complex carbs to achieve those results. The list contains all the food that is allowed on the DASH diet:

- Seafood
- Vegetables
- Lean meat
- Poultry
- Grains
- Seeds
- Fruits
- Low fat and non-fat dairy products
- Nuts

What Not To Eat

Any food that may cause hypertension, obesity, high blood pressure, and a spike in blood sugar levels is strictly prohibited on the DASH diet. You should cut the consumption of such food down to a minimum. The list of food that is not allowed on the DASH diet includes the following:

- Salt
- Salted Nuts
- Processed food
- Sugary beverages
- High-fat dairy products
- Excessive animal-based fats

Benefits of the DASH Diet

DASH diet remained associated with hypertension, prevention, and treatment for many years. But there were many studies on this diet that revealed that its constant and consistent consumption could also help you achieve other health advantages and an overall improvement in health.

Dash diet promotes the use of vegetables, grains, and fruits. It discourages saturated fats in any amount; therefore, it can effectively help keep the blood cholesterol levels controlled.

This diet provides a perfect serving-sized-based formula for daily food intake, perfect for shedding some extra pounds when followed by some daily exercise. Any diet that is good at controlling blood sugar and cholesterol levels while keeping the blood pressure in control is also great at preventing the risks of cardiac diseases. And DASH diet does the same for everyone. A human kidney suffers from damage or an excessive burden when forced to work against the mineral imbalance in the body. The perfect balance of sodium and potassium inside and outside the nephrons (the kidney cells) allows them to work with minimum damage. So, when you consume the DASH diet, your sodium and potassium intake is maintained, which keeps the kidneys healthy.

Lowering Your Blood Pressure

Blood pressure measures the systolic and diastolic blood pressure pumped out of a heart. According to the American Heart Association, a normal human systolic and diastolic pressure must be 120mmhg/80mmhg or less. Numbers higher than these are marked as elevated. Let me explain the numbers through a table here:

Category	Systolic Pressure (MM HG)	Diastolic Pressure (MM HG)
Normal Blood Pressure	120 or less	80 or less
Elevated Blood pressure	120-129	80
High Blood Pressure-Stage 1	130-139	80-89
High Blood Pressure-Stage 2	140 or higher	90 or higher
Critical State	180 or higher	120 or higher

High blood pressure or hypertension is a severe health condition. When left unchecked or untreated, it can cause serious health problems such as heart stroke, memory loss, cardiac arrest, kidney failure, etc. Anyone who experiences high blood pressure consistently must consult a doctor, take medication, and complement it with a diet that can control blood pressure. Bad cholesterol, thickening of the blood, aging, and electrolyte imbalance are prime factors responsible for causing high blood pressure.

Here is the list of non-medicinal ways to control your blood pressure levels.

Balance Diet

"A balanced diet is a healthy diet"; that axiom always stands to be true! Such a diet contains all the essential nutrients in an amount that is required by the body. The portion control suggested under the DASH diet is designed to balance the diet.

Less Sodium Intake

Our body has to retain more water to wash off extra sodium, which leads to high blood pressure. Daily consumption of 1500-2500mg sodium a day is safe to sustain normal blood pressure levels. By cutting salt from your diet and avoiding sodium-containing processed food products, you can do this. Many store-bought items contain high-sodium content, so make sure to read the labels and check their sodium content to decide. Buy sodium-free varieties of everyday spices, condiments, and seasonings.

Reduce Fat Intake

Saturated fats present in animal fat and dairy contain bad cholesterol, which is a low-density lipoprotein it tends to deposit in the blood vessels. This accumulation of cholesterol narrows down the vessels and increases blood pressure. Thus, a low-fat diet is excellent for keeping the blood vessels open.

Exercise

It is vital to release toxins out of the body and keep the body active. Exercise strengthens the mind and muscles of the body and helps burn off excessive fats. Daily exercise of 20-30 minutes is enough to keep you going. That may include cycling, walking, swimming, jogging, or any healthy physical activity.

Sleep Well

Sound sleep helps rejuvenate the body cells and keep the body's metabolism active. It is crucial to have 6-8 hours of sleep for a human adult.

Don't Smoke

Smoking is not only bad for the lungs, but it also affects the heart's health. Besides cancer-causing carcinogens, tobacco also contains nicotine which raises blood pressure.

Destress

Stress is never good for the body; it constricts the blood vessels, increasing blood pressure. Try relaxing your mind and body through breathing exercises, yoga, and meditation to de-stress.

Chapter 1: Breakfast Recipes

1. Egg Frittata

Prep time: 5 mins

Cooking time: 16 mins

Servings: 4

Ingredients:

- 4 eggs
- 3 tbsp. low-fat heavy cream
- 4 tbsp. grated cheddar cheese
- 4 mushrooms, sliced
- 3 cherry tomatoes halved
- 4 tbsp. chopped spinach
- 2 tbsp. fresh chopped herbs of choice
- 1 green onion, sliced

Directions:

1. Beat eggs with cream and the rest of the ingredients in a bowl.
2. At 350°F, preheat your air fryer.
3. Add egg mixture to a baking dish and air fry for 16 minutes.
4. Slice and serve.

Nutritional Facts: Calories 147; Fat 11g; Carbohydrate 3g; Protein 9g; Cholesterol 188mg; Sodium 133mg; Potassium 273mg

2. Ezekiel Bread Toast

Prep time: 10 mins

Cooking time: 10 mins

Servings: 2

Ingredients:

- 4 Ezekiel bread slices, cut diagonally in half
- 2 eggs
- ½ c. coconut milk
- 2 tbsp. coconut sugar
- 1 packet of stevia
- 1 tsp. vanilla
- 1 pinch cinnamon

To serve:

- Banana slices
- Maple Syrup
- Berries

Directions:

1. At 300°F, preheat your air fryer.
2. Beat eggs with coconut milk, coconut sugar, stevia, vanilla, and cinnamon in a shallow bowl.
3. Dip each bread slice in the egg-milk mixture.
4. Place the slices in the air fryer basket and air fry for 10 minutes.
5. Garnish and Serve.

Nutritional Facts: Calories 390; Fat 20.6g; Carbohydrate 39.1g; Protein 14.2g; Cholesterol 164mg; Sodium 335mg; Potassium 359mg

3. Blueberry Yogurt Pancakes

Prep time: 10 mins

Cooking time: 8 mins

Servings: 6

Ingredients:

- 2 large eggs
- 1 c. reduced-fat yogurt
- 4 tbsp. low-fat milk
- 3 tbsp. Peanut butter, melted
- ½ tsp. Lemon zest
- ½ tsp. vanilla extract
- ½ c. whole wheat flour
- ½ c. all-purpose flour
- ¼ c. barley flour
- 2 tbsp. sugar
- 1 tsp. baking powder
- 1 c. blueberries, rinsed and dried

Directions:

1. Beat egg with yogurt in a bowl.
2. Stir in melted butter, milk, and vanilla, then mix well.
3. Add flours, baking powder, and sugar, then mix until lump-free.
4. At 300°F, preheat your air fryer.
5. Take a suitable baking dish and grease it with cooking spray.
6. Divide the batter onto the baking dish ladle by ladle to make round pancakes.

7. Spread 2-3 berries on top of each pancake round.
8. Air Fry the pancakes for 4 minutes until golden brown.
9. Flip the pancake and continue to cook for 4 minutes.
10. Make more pancakes in the same way.
11. Serve.

Nutritional Facts: Calories 269; Fat 8.8g; Carbohydrate 38.9g; Protein 9.6g; Cholesterol 80mg; Sodium 98mg ; Potassium 130mg

4. Buckwheat Crepes

Prep time: 10 mins

Cooking time: 12 mins

Servings: 6

Ingredients:

- 1 c. un-toasted buckwheat flour
- ¾ tbsp. flaxseed meal
- 1 ¾ c. light (canned) coconut milk
- 1 tbsp. Avocado oil
- ⅛ tsp. ground cinnamon
- 1 tbsp. coconut sugar

Directions:

1. At 300°F, preheat your air fryer.
2. Blend buckwheat flour with sugar, coconut milk, cinnamon, avocado oil, and flaxseed meal in a mixing bowl until smooth and lump-free.
3. Pour ¼ cup of batter onto a parchment paper round.
4. Swirl the paper to spread the batter into a thin round crepe.
5. Cook for 3 minutes in the air fryer.
6. Transfer this crepe to a plate carefully, using a spatula.
7. Repeat the same with the rest of the batter to make more pancakes.
8. Serve the crepe with your favorite compote, jam, or fruits.

Nutritional Facts: Calories 251; Fat 18.3g; Carbohydrate 19.9g; Protein 5.2g; Cholesterol 0mg; Sodium 11mg ; Potassium 116mg

5. Blueberry Spelt Muffins

Prep time: 10 mins

Cooking time: 27 mins

Servings: 6

Ingredients:

- ¾ c. mashed ripe banana
- ¾ c. unsweetened almond milk
- 1 tsp. apple cider vinegar
- ¼ c. maple syrup
- 1 tsp. vanilla extract
- ¼ c. coconut oil, melted
- 2 c. white spelt flour
- 4 tbsp. coconut sugar
- 2 tsp. baking powder
- 1 ½ tsp. Cinnamon
- ½ tsp. baking soda
- ½ c. walnut halves, chopped
- 1 ¼ c. blueberries

Directions:

1. At 325°F, preheat your air fryer.
2. Grease 2 six-cup muffin trays with cooking spray and add a paper cup to each hole.
3. Mash bananas in a bowl, stir in vanilla, maple syrup, vinegar, and milk, then mix well.
4. Add baking soda, cinnamon, baking powder, sugar, and flour, then mix until lump-free.
5. Stir in melted coconut oil, then mix well.
6. Fold in blueberries and walnuts, then divide this batter into the greased muffin cups.
7. Air fry these blueberry muffins for 27 minutes until golden brown.
8. Allow them to cool first, then serve.

Nutritional Facts: Calories 374; Fat 16.6g; Carbohydrate 51.5g; Protein 8.4g; Cholesterol 0mg; Sodium 125mg; Potassium 301mg

6. Breakfast Cookies

Prep time: 10 mins
Cooking time: 16 mins
Servings: 12

Ingredients:

- 1 c. creamy peanut butter
- ¼ c. honey
- 1 tsp. vanilla extract
- 2 medium ripe bananas, mashed
- 1 tsp. ground cinnamon
- 2 ¼ c. quick oats, crushed
- ½ c. dried cranberries
- ⅔ c. chopped almonds

Directions:

1. At 300°F, preheat your air fryer.
2. Spread a parchment sheet on your baking dish and keep it aside.
3. Fix the paddle attachment in the stand mixer and mix peanut butter, cinnamon, banana, honey, and vanilla in this mixer.
4. Stir in oats, nuts, and dried cranberries.
5. Add ¼ cup of the prepared cookie dough mounds to the baking dish.
6. Air fry these breakfast cookies for 16 minutes in the preheated air fryer.
7. Allow them to cool first.
8. Serve.

Nutritional Facts: Calories 273; Fat 15.8g; Carbohydrate 27.5g; Protein 9g; Cholesterol 0mg; Sodium 151mg; Potassium 203mg

7. Morning Oats

Prep time: 15 mins.

Cooking time: 5 mins

Servings: 1

Ingredients:

- ½ c. unsweetened plain almond milk
- ¾ tbsp. chia seeds
- 2 tbsp. unsalted peanut butter
- 1 tbsp. maple syrup
- ½ c. gluten-free rolled oats

For the toppings:

- ¼ c. blueberries
- ¼ c. strawberries, sliced

Directions:

1. Add milk, chia seeds, peanut butter, and maple syrup to a baking dish.
2. Stir in oats and stir the mixture.
3. At 300°F, preheat your air fryer.
4. Place the oat dish in the air fryer basket and air fry for 5 minutes.
5. Garnish the oatmeal with berries.
6. Enjoy.

Nutritional Facts: Calories 456; Fat 26.1g; Carbohydrate 44.8g; Protein 14.5g; Cholesterol 0mg; Sodium 150mg; Potassium 291mg

8. Spinach Omelet

Prep time: 15 mins

Cooking time: 15 mins

Servings: 4

Ingredients:

- 4 eggs
- ½ c. shredded sharp cheddar cheese
- ¼ c. fresh spinach, chopped
- 2 scallions, chopped
- 2 tbsp. half and half
- Black pepper to taste

Directions:

1. Beat eggs with spinach and the rest of the ingredients in a bowl.
2. At 350°F, preheat your air fryer.
3. Add egg mixture to a baking dish and air fry for 10-15 minutes.
4. Slice and serve.

Nutritional Facts: Calories 368; Fat 3.4g; Carbohydrate 82.8g; Protein 16g; Cholesterol 2mg; Sodium 105mg; Potassium 191mg

9. Breakfast Quiches

Prep time: 10 mins

Cooking time: 16 mins

Servings: 6

Ingredients:

For the batter:

- ½ c. raw cashews
- 3 tbsp. Almond milk
- ½ tsp. hot sauce
- 1 tbsp. white miso paste
- 1 tsp. mustard
- 16 oz. super firm tofu
- 6 tbsp. Nutritional yeast flakes
- ½ tsp. Granulated onion
- ½ tsp. Paprika
- ½ tsp. Cumin
- ½ tsp. Ancho chili powder
- ⅛ tsp. Turmeric
- ½ tsp. canola oil

Add-Ons:

- ½ c. seitan bacon
- ½ c. red bell pepper chopped small
- ½ c. onions chopped small
- ½ c. curly kale chopped

Directions:

1. Soak cashews in water overnight, then drain.

2. At 330°F, preheat your air fryer.
3. Blend cashews with milk in a blender until smooth.
4. Stir in tofu and the rest of the ingredients, then blend until it makes a thick batter.
5. Fold in seitan bacon, pepper, onions, and kale, then mix well.
6. Divide the batter into greased mini muffin cups.
7. Place the muffin cups in the air fryer basket.
8. Air fry the quiches for 16 minutes in the preheated air fryer.
9. Serve.

Nutritional Facts: Calories 361; Fat 19g; Carbohydrate 24.4g; Protein 25.2g; Cholesterol 0mg; Sodium 74mg ; Potassium 126mg

10. Crusted French Toast

Prep time: 10 mins

Cooking time: 6 mins

Servings: 4

Ingredients:

- 1 c. rolled oats
- 1 c. pecans
- 2 tbsp. ground flax seed
- 1 tsp. ground cinnamon
- 8 pieces of whole-grain vegan bread
- ¾ c. almond milk
- Maple syrup, for serving

Directions:

1. At 350°F, preheat your air fryer.
2. Add cinnamon, flaxseed, nuts, and oats to a food processor and blend until crumbly.
3. Spread this mixture in a shallow pan.
4. Soak the bread in the milk for 15 seconds, then remove it.
5. Transfer the soaked bread to a baking pan suitable for the air fryer basket.
6. Spread the nutty mixture over the soaked bread.
7. Air fry the bread for 6 minutes in the preheated air fryer.
8. Serve with maple syrup on top.

Nutritional Facts: Calories 437; Fat 2.3g; Carbohydrate 42.7g; Protein 12.8g; Cholesterol 0mg; Sodium 18mg ; Potassium 46mg

Chapter 2: Snacks Recipes

11. Crispy Beans

Prep time: 10 mins

Cooking time: 20 mins

Servings: 4

Ingredients:

- 2 cans (15 oz.) of unsalted garbanzo beans
- ½ tsp. black pepper
- 1 tsp. garlic powder
- 1 tsp. onion powder
- 1 tsp. dried parsley flakes
- 2 tsp. dried dill
- Cooking spray

Directions:

1. At 400°F, preheat your air fryer.
2. Drain and rinse the beans in a strainer, then dry them with a kitchen towel.
3. Mix dill, parsley, onion powder, garlic powder, and black pepper in a small bowl.
4. Lightly grease a baking dish with cooking spray.
5. Spread the beans in the baking dish and grease the beans with cooking spray.
6. Drizzle the spice mixture over the beans and shake them to coat evenly.
7. Air fry the garbanzo beans for 20 minutes and shake after every 5 minutes.
8. Allow the beans to cool, then serve.

Nutritional Facts: Calories 64; Fat 1g; Carbohydrate 11.6g; Protein 3.7g; Cholesterol 0mg; Sodium 60mg ; Potassium 86mg

12. Onion Rings

Prep time: 10 mins

Cooking time: 15 mins

Servings: 6

Ingredients:

- 3 yellow onions

For the Wet Mix:

- ½ c. flour
- ⅔ c. almond milk
- ½ tsp. Paprika
- ¼ tsp. turmeric

For the Dry Mix:

- 1 c. panko breadcrumbs
- ½ tsp. Paprika
- ¼ tsp. turmeric

Directions:

1. At 400°F, preheat your Air fryer.
2. Mix flour with milk, paprika, and turmeric until smooth.
3. Toss breadcrumbs with turmeric and paprika in a bowl.
4. Cut the onions into ½ inch thick slices and separate them into rings.
5. Dip each ring in the flour batter and coat with the panko crumbs.
6. Place the onion rings in the air fryer basket and air fry for 15 minutes.

7. Flip the onion rings once cooked halfway through, then resume cooking.
8. Serve and enjoy.

Nutritional Facts: Calories 139; Fat 1.6g; Carbohydrate 27.7g; Protein 4g; Cholesterol 0mg; Sodium 82mg ; Potassium 106mg

13. Hummus

Prep time: 5 mins

Cooking time: 5 mins

Servings: 6

Ingredients:

- 1 c. canned garbanzo beans, drained
- 2 tbsp. lemon juice
- 2 tsp. vegetable oil
- ½ c. non-fat plain yogurt
- 1 garlic clove, chopped
- ¼ tsp. Black pepper
- ½ tsp. ground cumin
- 1 c. celery sticks

Directions:

1. At 300°F, preheat your air fryer.
2. Drain the garbanzo bean completely and spread them in the air fryer.
3. Air fry them for 5 minutes.

4. Blend beans with lemon juice, yogurt, garlic powder, black pepper, and cumin in a blender until smooth.
5. Transfer the hummus to a serving bowl.
6. Drizzle olive oil on top and serve the hummus with celery sticks.
7. Enjoy.

Nutritional Facts: Calories 153; Fat 3.9g; Carbohydrate 22.2g; Protein 7.7g; Cholesterol 1mg; Sodium 24mg ; Potassium 611mg

14. Sweet Potato Crisp

Prep time: 10 mins

Cooking time: 15 minutes

Servings: 4

Ingredients:

- 1 lb. sweet potato
- 2 tbsp. Olive oil
- ½ tsp. black pepper

Directions:

1. At 350°F, preheat your air fryer.
2. Use a mandolin to cut the sweet potato into thin slices.
3. Spread the sweet potatoes in the air fryer in a single layer.
4. Brush oil and sprinkle black pepper over the sweet potato slices and air fry for 15 minutes until crispy.
5. Flip the sweet potato slices once cooked halfway through, and cook in batches.
6. Allow them to cool, then serve.

Nutritional Facts: Calories 93; Fat 7g; Carbohydrate 8.4g; Protein 0.5g; Cholesterol 0mg; Sodium 11mg; Potassium 3mg

15. Cardamom Tea Cookies

Prep time: 10 mins

Cooking time: 10 mins

Servings: 8

Ingredients:

- 1 c. unsalted peanut butter
- 1 egg yolk
- ⅔ c. granulated sugar
- ½ tsp. ground cardamom
- ¼ tsp. baking soda
- 2 c. all-purpose flour

For the Coating:

- ⅓ c. granulated sugar

Directions:

1. At 350°F, preheat your air fryer.
2. Beat butter in an electric mixture for 30 seconds.
3. Add sugar and beat for 5 minutes on high speed until fluffy.
4. Add baking soda, egg yolk, and cardamom, then mix well.
5. Slowly add flour while beating the mixture and mix until it makes a dough.
6. Cover and refrigerate this dough for 30 minutes.

7. Make 1-inch balls out of this cardamom dough and place these balls in the air fryer basket in batches.
8. Press the balls into cookies and air fry for 10 minutes.
9. Coat the cookies with the rest of the sugar.
10. Allow the cookie to cool, then serve.

Nutritional Facts: Calories 387; Fat 23.9g; Carbohydrate 40.7g; Protein 3.8g; Cholesterol 87mg; Sodium 277mg; Potassium 391mg

16. Whole-Wheat Pretzel

Prep time: 10 mins

Cooking time: 16 mins

Servings: 12

Ingredients:

- 1 package of active dry yeast
- 2 tsp. brown sugar
- 1 ½ c. warm water
- 1 c. bread flour
- 3 c. whole-wheat flour
- 1 tbsp. olive oil
- ½ c. wheat gluten
- Cooking spray
- ¼ c. baking soda
- 1 egg white

Directions:

1. Mix 2 teaspoons of sugar, yeast, and warm water in a food processor.
2. Leave this mixture for 5 minutes.
3. Stir in gluten, olive oil, and flours, then mix to make a smooth dough.
4. Knead the prepared dough on a working surface for 1 minute.
5. Transfer it to a greased bowl, spray cooking oil on top, and cover it with a plastic sheet.

6. Keep this dough in a warm place in the kitchen for 1 hour.
7. Punch dough the raised dough, then cut it into 12 equal-sized pieces.
8. Roll each piece into a rope and keep them aside.
9. Take a dough rope and shape it into a U shape.
10. Now hold the two ends of the U and cross them while moving them towards the bottom of the U.
11. Pinch each end under the bottom to make a pretzel shape.
12. Repeat the same with the remaining dough ropes as well.
13. Boil ten cups in a large cooking pot and add ¼ cup baking soda.
14. Dip each pretzel in this water for 30 seconds, then immediately transfer to a suitable baking sheet lined with parchment paper.
15. At 400°F, preheat your air fryer.
16. Brush the top of the prepared pretzel with beaten egg white.
17. Air Fry each pretzel for 15 minutes.
18. Serve.

Nutritional Facts: Calories 167; Fat 2.4g; Carbohydrate 30.7g; Protein 8.3g; Cholesterol 0mg; Sodium 360mg; Potassium 285mg

17. Mini-Meatballs

Prep time: 10 mins

Cooking time: 25 mins

Servings: 6

Ingredients:

- 1 lb. lean ground pork
- 2 tbsp. chopped fresh cilantro
- 1½ tbsp. lime juice
- 1-piece (2") ginger, grated
- 1 carrot, shredded
- Black pepper, to taste

Directions:

1. At 375°F, preheat your air fryer.
2. Spread a parchment paper on a suitable baking dish.
3. Mix pork with cilantro, lime juice, ginger, carrot, and black pepper in a bowl.
4. Make 1 ½ inches round balls out of this mixture and place them in the baking dish.
5. Air fry these meatballs for 20-25 minutes.
6. Insert a toothpick into each meatball.
7. Serve.

Nutritional Facts: Calories 116; Fat 2.7g; Carbohydrate 2.1g; Protein 19.9g; Cholesterol 55mg; Sodium 51mg ; Potassium 367mg

18. Potato Pancakes

Prep time: 10 mins

Cooking time: 5 mins

Servings: 6

Ingredients:

- 6 potatoes, peeled, cooked, and mashed
- 2 eggs
- ¼ c. seasoned bread crumbs
- 1 tbsp. parsley
- ¼ c. flour

Directions:

1. At 400°F, preheat your air fryer.
2. Mix breadcrumbs, eggs, parsley, and potatoes in a large bowl.
3. Make six small ovals out of this mixture.
4. Roll them in the flour and keep them aside.
5. Air fry the potato cakes for 5 minutes until golden brown.
6. Serve.

Nutritional Facts: Calories 313; Fat 14.1g; Carbohydrate 41g; Protein 6.7g; Cholesterol 55mg; Sodium 122mg; Potassium 341mg

19. Spiced Pita Chips

Prep time: 10 mins

Cooking time: 10 mins

Servings: 6

Ingredients:

- 1 tbsp. dried Italian seasoning
- 1 tbsp. Low-fat Parmesan cheese, grated
- ¼ tsp. garlic powder
- 2 (6-inch) whole-wheat pita bread
- Cooking spray

Directions:

1. At 350°F, preheat your air fryer.
2. Mix Italian seasoning, garlic powder, and parmesan in a bowl.
3. Cut each pita into eight equal-sized wedges and separate each wedge into two pieces.
4. Spread a parchment sheet in the air fryer basket.
5. Spread the pita wedges in the basket in a single layer.
6. Spray the pita pieces with cooking spray.
7. Drizzle the parmesan mixture on top and air fry for 10 minutes.
8. Allow the chips to cool.
9. Serve.

Nutritional Facts: Calories 79; Fat 2.3g; Carbohydrate 12.3g; Protein 3.6g; Cholesterol 5mg; Sodium 351mg; Potassium 398mg

20. Zucchini Chips

Prep time: 10 mins

Cooking time: 20 mins.

Servings: 4

Ingredients:

- 1 large zucchini
- 2 Tbsp. olive oil

Directions:

1. At 325°F, preheat your air fryer.
2. Use a mandolin to cut the zucchini into thin slices.
3. Spread the zucchini slices in the air fryer basket into a single layer.
4. Brush oil over the zucchini slices and air fry for 20 minutes until crispy and brown.
5. Flip the zucchini slices once cooked halfway through.
6. Allow them to cool, then serve.

Nutritional Facts: Calories 73; Fat 7.2g; Carbohydrate 2.7g; Protein 1g; Cholesterol 0mg; Sodium 8mg; Potassium 242mg

Chapter 3: Salads Recipes

21. Black Bean Salad

Prep time: 10 mins

Cooking time: 5 mins

Servings: 8

Ingredients:

- ½ c. red onion, sliced
- 1 ripe avocado, pitted and chopped
- ¼ c. cilantro leaves
- ¼ c. lime juice
- 2 tbsp. olive oil
- 1 garlic clove, minced
- 8 c. mixed salad greens
- 2 c. frozen corn, thawed
- 1 pt. grape tomatoes halved
- 1 (15 oz.) can of low-sodium black beans, rinsed

Directions:

1. At 300°F, preheat your air fryer.
2. Spread the rinsed black beans in the air fryer and air fry for 5 minutes.
3. Add sliced onion to a medium bowl and pour enough cold water to cover it.
4. Soak it for 5 minutes, then drain.
5. Blend avocado with garlic, oil, lime juice, and cilantro in a food processor for 2 minutes.
6. Mix beans with tomatoes, corn, greens, and onion.
7. Fold in avocado dressing, then mix well with a spatula.
8. Serve.

Nutritional Facts: Calories 330; Fat 9.7g; Carbohydrate 50.2g; Protein 15.3g; Cholesterol 0mg; Sodium 165mg; Potassium 472mg

22. Green Salad With Chickpeas

Prep time: 10 mins

Cooking time: 5 mins

Servings: 6

Ingredients:

For the Dressing:

- 1 avocado, peeled and pitted
- 1 ½ c. low-fat buttermilk
- ¼ c. fresh herbs, chopped
- 2 tbsp. rice vinegar

For the Salad:

- 2 c. romaine lettuce, chopped
- 1 c. bean sprouts
- 1 c. cucumber, julienned
- 1 (15 oz.) can of chickpeas, rinsed
- ¼ c. low-fat Swiss cheese, diced
- 6 cherry tomatoes, chopped

Directions:

1. At 350°F, preheat your air fryer.
2. Spread the chickpeas in the air fryer basket and air fry for 5 minutes.
3. Blend avocado, vinegar, herbs, and buttermilk in a blender until smooth.
4. Toss cucumber with lettuce in a salad bowl and pour ¼ cup of dressing on top.
5. Add tomatoes, cheese, and chickpeas on top.
6. Garnish with bean sprouts.
7. Serve.

Nutritional Facts: Calories 407; Fat 13.8g; Carbohydrate 54g; Protein 19.8g; Cholesterol 8mg; Sodium 276mg; Potassium 612mg

23. Spinach Salad With Maple Dressing

Prep time: 10 mins

Cooking time: 10 mins

Servings: 6

Ingredients:

- 2 c. mature spinach leaves, torn
- 2 tbsp. olive oil
- 1 c. lettuce, torn
- 1 medium shallot, chopped
- ¼ c. cider vinegar
- 2 tbsp. pure maple syrup
- ¼ tsp. black pepper
- 1 c. cherry tomatoes, halved
- ¼ c. smoked low-fat cheese, diced
- ¼ c. pecans

Directions:

1. At 400°F, preheat your air fryer.
2. Line the air fryer basket with parchment paper.
3. Spread pecans in the air fryer and air fry for 5 minutes.
4. Toss tomato, lettuce, and spinach in a salad bowl and keep it aside.
5. Sauté shallot with oil in a small skillet for 5 minutes.
6. Stir in maple syrup, vinegar, and black pepper, then cook to a boil.
7. Pour this dressing over the spinach salad and garnish with pecans and cheese.
8. Serve.

Nutritional Facts: Calories 149; Fat 11.9g; Carbohydrate 8.7g; Protein 4g; Cholesterol 1mg; Sodium 78mg ; Potassium 413mg

24. Broccoli Salad

Prep time: 5 mins

Cooking time: 6 mins

Servings: 6

Ingredients:

- 2 heads of broccoli, cut into florets
- 2 tsp. olive oil
- ½ c. almonds
- ¼ c. dried cranberries
- 1 tbsp. fresh dill, chopped
- 4 very thin slices of lemon

For the Lemony Dressing:

- ¼ c. lemon juice
- 1 tbsp. maple syrup
- 1 tsp. Dijon mustard
- 1 tsp. balsamic vinegar
- 1 garlic clove, grated
- 2 tbsp. olive oil

Directions:

1. At 350°F, preheat your Air fryer.
2. Toss broccoli florets with oil in the air fryer basket.
3. Air fry them for 6 minutes in the air fryer basket.
4. Mix lemon juice, maple syrup, Dijon mustard, vinegar, garlic, and olive oil in a salad bowl.
5. Toss in the broccoli, almond, dill, cranberries, and lemon slices.
6. Mix well and serve

Nutritional Facts: Calories 203; Fat 10.7g; Carbohydrate 18.7g; Protein 5.2g; Cholesterol 25mg; Sodium 55mg ; Potassium 315mg

25. Radish Couscous Salad

Prep time: 5 mins

Cooking time: 5 mins

Servings: 2

Ingredients:

- 2 tbsp. lime juice
- 2 tsp. distilled white vinegar
- 2 tsp. ground cumin
- 2 c. couscous, cooked
- 1 c. chickpeas, cooked
- 1 c. fresh parsley, chopped
- ⅔ c. pomegranate seeds
- ½ c. radishes, sliced
- 2 c. baby spinach

Directions:

1. At 300°F, preheat your air fryer.
2. Spread the chickpeas in the air fryer basket and air fry for 5 minutes.
3. Mix cumin, vinegar, and lime juice in a salad bowl.
4. Toss in couscous, chickpeas, parsley, pomegranate seeds, and radishes.
5. Mix the veggies with the dressing well.
6. Spread spinach on a platter and add the remaining salad on top.
7. Serve.

Nutritional Facts: Calories 193; Fat 1.7g; Carbohydrate 37.6g; Protein 8g; Cholesterol 0mg; Sodium 35mg; Potassium 412mg

26. Brussels Sprout Salad

Prep time: 10 mins

Cooking time: 7 mins

Servings: 4

Ingredients:

- 4 c. Brussels sprouts
- 1 onion, shredded
- ¼ c. olive oil
- ¼ c. fresh lemon juice
- ½ c. pine nuts, toasted
- ⅓ c. dried cranberries
- ⅓ c. chopped chives
- Black pepper, to taste

Directions:

1. At 400°F, preheat your Air fryer.
2. Toss Brussel sprouts with 2 tablespoons of oil in a bowl.
3. Spread the Brussel sprouts in the Air fryer basket.
4. Air fry them for 7 minutes and shake once cooked halfway through.
5. Meanwhile, toss all the salad ingredients in a suitable salad bowl.
6. Serve fresh.

Nutritional Facts: Calories 281; Fat 26.6g; Carbohydrate 14.4g; Protein 2.7g; Cholesterol 0mg; Sodium 186mg; Potassium 286mg

27. Spinach Salad With Roasted Sweet Potatoes

Prep time: 10 mins

Cooking time: 18 mins

Servings: 4

Ingredients:

- 1 sweet potato, peeled and diced
- 5 tbsp. Extra-virgin olive oil
- ½ tsp. ground black pepper
- ½ c. packed fresh basil leaves
- 3 tbsp. cider vinegar
- 1 tbsp. shallot, chopped
- 2 tsp. whole-grain mustard
- 10 c. baby spinach
- 1 (15 oz.) can of low-sodium cannellini beans, rinsed
- 2 c. cabbage, shredded
- 1 c. red bell pepper. chopped
- ⅓ c. chopped pecans, toasted

Directions:

1. At 400°F, preheat your air fryer.
2. Mix sweet potatoes with ¼ teaspoon of black pepper and one tablespoon of oil in a large bowl.
3. Spread the potatoes in the air fryer basket and air fry for 18 minutes.
4. Blend basil, vinegar, remaining ¼ cup of oil, shallot, ¼ teaspoon of black pepper, and mustard in a small food processor until smooth.
5. Toss spinach with sweet potatoes, bell pepper, cabbage, beans, and pecans in a salad bowl.
6. Drizzle the prepared dressing on top.
7. Serve.

Nutritional Facts: Calories 370; Fat 30.6g; Carbohydrate 21.5g; Protein 7.4g; Cholesterol 0mg; Sodium 261mg; Potassium 382mg

28. Mushroom Salad

Prep time: 10 mins

Cooking time: 4 mins

Servings: 2

Ingredients:

- 1 lb. fresh mushroom, sliced
- 1 red bell pepper
- 2 tsp. olive oil
- 2 tsp. dried parsley
- 2 tbsp. dried dill
- 1 tbsp. lemon juice
- 1 tbsp. white wine vinegar
- Black pepper, to taste

Directions:

1. At 300°F, preheat your air fryer.
2. Toss mushrooms with the rest of the salad ingredients in a baking dish.
3. Air fry this salad for 4 minutes.
4. Serve.

Nutritional Facts: Calories 110; Fat 5.5g; Carbohydrate 12.2g; Protein 7.8g; Cholesterol 0mg; Sodium 16mg; Potassium 847mg

29. Napa Cabbage Salad

Prep time: 10 mins

Cooking time: 2 min

Servings: 4

Ingredients:

- 2 tbsp. rice vinegar
- 1 tbsp. honey
- 1 tbsp. canola oil
- 1 ½ tbsp. low-sodium soy sauce
- 1 package of ramen noodles
- 1 tbsp. sliced almonds
- 1 small head of napa cabbage, shredded
- 1 carrot, spiralized
- Greens, to garnish

Directions:

1. At 300°F, preheat your air fryer.
2. Spread the noodles and almonds in the air fryer basket and air fry for 2 minutes.
3. Mix soy sauce, oil, honey, and vinegar in a small saucepan.
4. Cook this dressing to a boil, then remove it from the heat.
5. Transfer the almond noodle mixture to a salad bowl.
6. Add carrot, cabbage, and the prepared dressing.
7. Mix well and garnish
8. Serve.

Nutritional Facts: Calories 228; Fat 9.2g; Carbohydrate 33g; Protein 6.5g; Cholesterol 0mg; Sodium 246mg; Potassium 152mg

30. Bean Avocado Salad

Prep time: 10 mins

Cooking time: 5 mins

Servings: 4

Ingredients:

- 1 c. white beans, cooked
- 1 c. red beans, cooked
- 1 red apple, chopped
- ½ avocado, diced
- ¼ c. parsley, chopped
- ½ tsp. cumin
- ½ tsp. chili powder
- ½ tsp. dried oregano
- 2 tsp. lime juice
- Black pepper, to taste

Directions:

1. At 300°F, preheat your air fryer.
2. Spread the rinsed white and red beans in the air fryer basket and air fry for 5 minutes.
3. Mix the air-fried beans with the rest of the salad ingredients in a salad bowl.
4. Refrigerate this salad for 15 minutes, then serve.

Nutritional Facts: Calories 208; Fat 5.6g; Carbohydrate 33.7g; Protein 9.1g; Cholesterol 0mg; Sodium 118mg; Potassium 671mg

Chapter 4: Soups Recipes

31. Spicy Sweet Potato Soup

Prep time: 10 mins

Cooking time: 20 mins

Servings: 4

Ingredients:

- 3 sweet potatoes, peeled, diced
- 1 onion, chopped
- 4 c. low-sodium chicken broth
- 2 garlic cloves, chopped
- 1 tsp. gingerroot, grated
- 2 tbsp. unsalted peanut butter
- 1 ½ tbsp. lime juice
- 1 tbsp. canola oil
- ¼ tsp. ground cumin
- ⅛ tsp. cayenne pepper
- 1 tomato, chopped
- 2 tbsp. fresh cilantro, chopped
- Black pepper to taste

Directions:

1. At 300°F, preheat your air fryer.
2. Spread sweet potatoes in the air fryer basket and air fry for 15 minutes.
3. Sauté chopped onion and garlic with oil in a large saucepan for 5 minutes over medium heat.
4. Stir in broth, cayenne pepper, cumin, grated ginger, and sweet potatoes, then cook to a boil.
5. Blend this soup in a blender until smooth, then return to the saucepan.
6. Add lime juice and peanut butter, then ladle into the serving bowl.
7. Garnish with cilantro and tomato.
8. Serve.

Nutritional Facts: Calories 274; Fat 9.3g; Carbohydrate 40g; Protein 9.4g; Cholesterol 0mg; Sodium 453mg; Potassium 457mg

32. Barley Carrot Soup

Prep time: 15 mins

Cooking time: 70 mins

Servings: 4

Ingredients:

- 1 yellow onion, chopped
- 2 garlic cloves, chopped
- 2 tbsp. olive oil
- ½ lb. carrots, chopped
- 1 (28oz.) can of diced tomatoes
- 1 c. pearled barley
- ½ lb. boneless lean beef, diced
- ½ tsp dried basil
- ½ tsp dried oregano
- Black pepper, to taste
- 6 c. vegetable broth
- 1 russet potato, diced
- 1 tbsp. lemon juice
- 1 handful of fresh parsley, chopped

Directions:

1. At 375°F, preheat your air fryer.
2. Season the lean beef with black pepper.
3. Place it in the air fryer basket and spray with cooking spray.
4. Air fry the beef for 20-25 minutes until tender, then shred and keep the meat aside.
5. Sauté carrot, garlic, and onion with oil and oil in a saucepan for 5 minutes.
6. Stir in tomatoes, meat, and the rest of the soup ingredients.
7. Cover and cook this soup on a simmer for 45 minutes
8. Stir in black pepper, then mix well.

9. Serve.

Nutritional Facts: Calories 154; Fat 6.5g; Carbohydrate 15.7g; Protein 20.6g; Cholesterol 16mg; Sodium 167mg, Potassium 401mg

33. Cream Of Mushroom Soup

Prep time: 15 mins

Cooking time: 21 mins

Servings: 2

Ingredients:

- 1 tbsp. unsalted butter
- 4 oz. baby Bella mushrooms, sliced
- ½ c. button mushrooms, sliced
- 1 c. unsalted chicken broth
- ½ tsp. Onion powder
- ⅛ tsp. Dried thyme
- ¼ tsp. garlic powder
- ½ c. fat-free milk
- ¼ c. all-purpose flour
- Black pepper to taste

Directions:

1. At 350°F, preheat your air fryer.
2. Season the button mushrooms with black pepper.
3. Spread these mushrooms in the air fryer basket.
4. Air fry them for 15 minutes until brown and crispy.
5. Sauté Bella mushrooms with butter with in a medium saucepan for 5 minutes.
6. Stir in garlic powder, onion powder, and chicken broth.
7. Reduce its heat to a simmer and cook for 5 minutes.
8. Mix milk with flour in a bowl and pour into the soup.
9. Stir and cook this soup for 1 minute until it thickens, then puree it in a blender.
10. Garnish with air-fried mushrooms.

11. Serve.

Nutritional Facts: Calories 169; Fat 7.2g; Carbohydrate 18.2g; Protein 6.8g; Cholesterol 20mg; Sodium 53mg ; Potassium 79mg

34. Carrot Ginger Soup

Prep time: 15 mins

Cooking time: 20 mins

Servings: 4

Ingredients:

- 1 tbsp. unsalted butter
- 1 large white onion, chopped
- 3 c. reduced-sodium vegetable broth
- 1 lb. peeled baby carrots
- 1 tbsp. fresh ginger, grated
- ¼ c. reduced-fat sour cream
- White pepper to taste
- 2 tbsp. fresh micro greens

Directions:

1. At 350°F, preheat your air fryer.
2. Spread the baby carrots in the air fryer basket and air fry for 10-15 minutes until tender.
3. Sauté onions with butter in a saucepan for 5 minutes.
4. Stir in ginger, then cook to a boil.
5. Stir in carrots and sour cream and puree the soup in a blender until smooth.
6. Adjust seasoning with white pepper, then ladle into the serving bowl.
7. Garnish with chives.
8. Enjoy.

Nutritional Facts: Calories 144; Fat 6.6g; Carbohydrate 19.5g; Protein 3.1g; Cholesterol 8mg; Sodium 229mg; Potassium 311mg

35. Sweet Potato Lentil Soup

Prep time: 10 mins

Cooking time: 31 mins

Servings: 4

Ingredients:

- 1 tbsp. olive oil
- 1 medium white onion, peeled and diced
- 1 sweet potato, quartered
- 1 medium carrot, diced
- 5 cloves of garlic, peeled and minced
- 6 c. vegetable stock
- 1 ½ c. red lentils, rinsed and picked over
- ⅔ c. whole-kernel corn
- 2 tsp. ground cumin
- 1 tsp. curry powder
- 1 pinch each of saffron and cayenne
- Zest and juice of 1 small lemon
- Black pepper, to taste

Directions:

1. At 350°F, preheat your air fryer.
2. Spread the sweet potatoes in the air fryer basket.
3. Spray with cooking spray and the air fryer for 10 minutes.
4. Sauté onion and carrots with oil in a stockpot for 5 minutes over medium-high heat.
5. Stir in garlic and cook for 1 minute.
6. Add stock, curry powder, cumin, corn, and lentils, then cover and cook for 15 minutes.
7. Stir in sweet potatoes, then puree this soup with a blender until smooth.
8. Adjust seasoning with lemon zest and black pepper.

9. Garnish and serve.

Nutritional Facts: Calories 338; Fat 4.9g; Carbohydrate 54g; Protein 20.6g; Cholesterol 0mg; Sodium 106mg; Potassium 867mg

36. Cauliflower Soup

Prep time: 10 mins

Cooking time: 49 mins

Servings: 2

Ingredients:

For the Cauliflower Soup:

- 2 tbsp. olive oil
- 1 medium onion, sliced
- 2 garlic cloves, chopped
- 1 head of cauliflower, cut into florets
- 2 sprigs of fresh thyme
- 4 c. low-sodium vegetable stock
- Black pepper, to taste

For the Toppings:

- Fresh thyme finely chopped
- Extra virgin olive oil

For the Roasted Chickpeas:

- 1 can (14 oz.) can chickpeas, drained
- 1 tbsp. olive oil
- 1 tsp. Paprika
- ½ tsp. Chili powder

- ¼ tsp. cumin

Directions:

1. At 350°F, preheat your air fryer.
2. Toss chickpeas with cumin, chili powder, paprika, and oil in a bowl.
3. Spread the chickpeas in the air fryer basket and air fry for 20-25 minutes until golden brown.
4. Sauté onion with oil in a large pot over medium-high heat for 5 minutes.
5. Stir in garlic and cook for 1 minute.
6. Toss in chopped cauliflower and thyme, then cook for 3 minutes.
7. Pour in vegetable stock and cook on a simmer for 15 minutes.
8. Adjust seasoning with black pepper, then puree this soup in a blender until smooth.
9. Garnish the soup with roasted chickpeas.
10. Serve.

Nutritional Facts: Calories 250; Fat 15.2g; Carbohydrate 25.2g; Protein 7.3g; Cholesterol 0mg; Sodium 259mg; Potassium 211mg

37. Butternut Squash Soup

Prep time: 10 mins

Cooking time: 25 mins

Servings: 4

Ingredients:

- 1 ½ lb. butternut squash, peeled and diced
- 2 medium carrots, cut into 1 ½-inch piece
- 1 orange bell pepper, cut into 1-inch-thick slices
- ½ medium onion, cut into 4 wedges
- 3 tbsp. olive oil
- ¾ tsp. granulated garlic
- ½ tsp. ground ginger
- ¼ tsp. dried thyme
- Black pepper, to taste
- 3 c. low-sodium vegetable broth
- ½ c. low-fat heavy cream
- Finely chopped chives for serving

Directions:

1. At 375°F, preheat your air fryer.
2. Toss the butternut squash, bell pepper, onion, carrots, granulated garlic, olive oil, ginger, thyme, and several grinds of black pepper together in a large bowl
3. Spread the squash mixture in the air fryer basket and air fry for 20 minutes.
4. Puree the veggies with the rest of the ingredients in a blender until smooth.
5. Add the soup to a pot and cook for 5 minutes.
6. Garnish and serve warm.

Nutritional Facts: Calories 236; Fat 11.2g; Carbohydrate 13.6g; Protein 19.7g; Cholesterol 40mg; Sodium 78mg ; Potassium 116mg

38. Lentil Chicken Soup

Prep time: 15 mins

Cooking time: 2 hrs. 26 mins

Servings: 4

Ingredients:

- ½ lb. boneless chicken breasts
- 2 tbsp. olive oil
- 1 medium yellow onion, chopped
- 4 garlic cloves, minced
- 1 medium yellow bell pepper, chopped
- 1 medium red bell pepper, chopped
- 2 c. red lentils, rinsed
- 2 c. water
- 1 tsp. cumin ground
- ¾ tsp. black pepper
- 2 c. low-sodium vegetable broth
- ½ c. cilantro, chopped
- 2 limes, juiced

Directions:

1. Rub chicken with 1 tbsp oil and place it in the air fryer basket,
2. Air fry the chicken for 20 minutes and flip once cooked halfway through.
3. Shred the cooked chicken once cooled, and then keep it aside.
4. Sauté onions with peppers and oil in a large skillet for 5 minutes on medium-high heat.
5. Stir in garlic and sauté for 1 minute.
6. Transfer this mixture to a slow cooker and add red lentils, water, chicken, broth, lime juice, black pepper, and cumin; then cover and cook for 4 hours on low heat or 2 hours on high heat.
7. Garnish with cilantro and serve.

Nutritional Facts: Calories 410; Total Fat 4.7g; Carbohydrate 64.8g; Protein 27.6g; Cholesterol 0mg; Sodium 86mg; Potassium 1043mg

39. French Onion Soup

Prep time: 15 mins

Cooking time: 1 hr. 57 mins

Servings: 8

Ingredients:

- 4 large onions, peeled and sliced
- ½ tsp. brown sugar
- 6 tbsp. unsalted butter
- 8 c. beef broth, no salt added
- ⅓ c. dry white table wine
- ½ tsp. thyme ground dry
- 2 bay leaves
- ½ tsp. black pepper
- 2 tbsp. low-sodium Worcestershire sauce
- 1 tsp. liquid smoke
- 1 tsp. garlic powder
- 2 tsp. herb ox beef bouillon no-sodium granules
- 1 tsp. kitchen bouquet browning and seasoning sauce
- 2 c. low-fat Swiss gruyere cheese, shredded

Directions:

1. Sauté sliced onion with butter in a large skillet for 50 minutes on medium-low heat until golden brown.
2. Add the rest of the onion soup ingredients except the bread and cheese.
3. Cook this soup to a boil, then reduce the heat to a simmer and cook for 1 hour.
4. Remove and discard the bay leaf.
5. Brush a low-sodium bread with olive oil and place it in the air fryer basket.
6. Air fry this bread for 5 minutes.
7. Divide the soup into the serving ramekins and top each with bread and cheese.
8. Place the ramekins in the air fryer one at a time and air fry for 2-3 minutes until the cheese is melted.

9. Serve warm.

Nutritional Facts: Calories 246; Fat 18g; Carbohydrate 7.1g; Protein 11.6g; Cholesterol 53mg; Sodium 318mg; Potassium 214mg

40. Turkey Noodle Soup

Prep time: 15 mins

Cooking time: 40 mins

Servings: 6

Ingredients:

- 6 c. low-sodium turkey stock
- 1 bay leaf
- 1 c. carrot, sliced
- ¾ c. onion, chopped
- ¾ c. celery, diced
- 2 garlic cloves, minced
- Black pepper, to taste
- ¼ c. parsley, chopped
- 3 oz. low-sodium egg noodles
- 2 c. boneless turkey breast, diced
- 1 spring onion, green part, chopped

Directions:

1. At 350°F, preheat your air fryer.
2. Place the turkey pieces in the air fryer basket and spray with cooking spray.
3. Air fry the turkey for 20 minutes until tender, then shred the cooked meat.
4. Add turkey stock, bay leaf, onion, carrots, garlic, black pepper, and celery to a large saucepan and cook for 15 minutes on a simmer.
5. Stir in shredded turkey, noodles, and parsley, then cook for 5 minutes.
6. Remove and discard the bay leaf.
7. Garnish with green onion.

8. Serve warm.

Nutritional Facts: Calories 217; Fat 2.9g; Carbohydrate 17.4g; Protein 30.2g; Cholesterol 80mg; Sodium 223mg; Potassium 124mg

Chapter 5: Poultry Recipes

41. Chicken Zucchini Skewers

Prep time: 10 mins

Cooking time: 10 mins

Servings: 4

Ingredients:

For the Marinade:

- 1 tbsp. vegetable oil
- 1 tbsp. sesame oil
- 2 garlic cloves, peeled and minced
- 1 tsp. minced ginger
- 1 tbsp. apple cider vinegar
- 1 tbsp. low-sodium dark soy sauce
- 3 tbsp. honey

For the Skewers:

- 2 chicken breasts, diced
- 1 red bell pepper, cut into large chunks
- 1 zucchini, sliced
- 1 onion, peeled and cut into squares

Directions:

1. Mix chicken cubes with vegetable oil, sesame oil, garlic, vinegar, ginger, soy sauce, and honey in a bowl.
2. Cover and refrigerate this chicken for 20 minutes.
3. Add the veggies to the chicken and the marinade, then mix well to coat.
4. Thread the chicken, zucchini, red bell pepper, and onion on wooden skewers.
5. At 350°F, preheat your air fryer.
6. Air fry the chicken skewers for 10 minutes and flip them once cooked halfway through.
7. Serve warm.

Nutritional Facts: Calories 551; Fat 24.4g; Carbohydrate 41g; Protein 43.8g; Cholesterol 125mg; Sodium 266mg; Potassium 830mg

42. Saucy Duck Breast

Prep time: 15 mins

Cooking time: 20 mins

Servings: 6

Ingredients:

- 3 (1 lb. each) Muscovy duck breasts
- 1 tbsp. crushed black peppercorns
- 4 garlic cloves, sliced
- 2 tbsp. unsalted butter
- 1 large shallot, sliced
- 1 tbsp. tomato paste
- 2 c. unsalted chicken broth
- 2 tbsp. red wine
- 1 tbsp. Cognac or brandy
- 2 tsp. potato starch

Directions:

1. Season the duck breasts with peppercorns and garlic, then refrigerate for 1 hour.
2. At 350°F, preheat your air fryer.
3. Place the duck in the air fryer basket and cook for 15 minutes.
4. Sauté shallot with butter in a skillet for 1 minute.
5. Stir in garlic and sauté for 1 minute.
6. Add tomato paste, chicken broth, red wine, and cognac.
7. Mix well and cook on a simmer for 5 minutes.
8. Stir potato starch with 2 teaspoons of water in a bowl and pour it into the sauce.
9. Cook until the sauce thickens.

10. Slice the duck and serve with sauce on top.

Nutritional Facts: Calories 240; Fat 6.1g; Carbohydrate 31.6g; Protein 10.1g; Cholesterol 42mg; Sodium 318mg; Potassium 201mg

43. Chicken Wraps

Prep time: 15 mins

Cooking time: 10 mins

Servings: 2

Ingredients:

- 1 boneless chicken breast, cut into strips
- 1 red bell pepper, cut into strips
- 1 onion, cut into strips
- ¼ tsp. garlic, minced
- 1 tbsp. olive oil
- 1 tsp. dried parsley
- 1 tsp. curry powder
- 1 lemon, juiced
- 2 pita rounds
- Lemon wedges to serve

Directions:

1. Mix chicken with curry powder, lemon juice, and the rest of the ingredients.
2. Layer the air fryer basket with parchment paper.
3. Spread the chicken mixture in the air fryer basket.
4. Air fry it for 10 minutes and shake once cooked halfway through.
5. Divide the chicken mixture into the pita rounds.
6. Roll and serve with lemon wedges.

Nutritional Facts: Calories 208; Fat 7.1g; Carbohydrate 24.1g; Protein 14.1g; Cholesterol 31mg; Sodium 203mg; Potassium 266mg

44. Roasted Chicken

Prep time: 15 mins

Cooking time: 40 mins

Servings: 6

Ingredients:

- 1 whole chicken weighing about 2 lbs.
- 1 tsp. ground Coriander
- 1 tsp. paprika powder
- 1 tsp. chili powder
- 1 tsp. dried mint
- 1 tsp. dried basil
- Cilantro for serving, chopped

Directions:

1. Mix coriander, paprika, chili powder, mint, and basil in a bowl.
2. Cut the whole chicken breast like a butterfly.
3. At 350°F, preheat your air fryer.
4. Place the chicken in a roast pan with the open side down.
5. Rub the prepared spice mixture on top and air fry for 35-40 minutes.
6. Flip the chicken once cooked halfway through.
7. Serve warm.

Nutritional Facts: Calories 563; Fat 37.5g; Carbohydrate 0.5g; Protein 56.1g; Cholesterol 213mg; Sodium 218mg; Potassium 19mg

45. Chicken Brats

Prep time: 10 mins

Cooking time: 11 mins

Servings: 4

Ingredients:

- 1 c. yellow onion, minced
- 4 garlic cloves, minced
- ½ tsp. canola oil
- 1 c. brown rice, cooked
- 1 lb. ground chicken breast
- 2 tsp. fennel seed
- 1 tsp. cumin seed
- 1 tsp. ground paprika
- 1 tsp. Ground black pepper
- ½ tsp. Ground white pepper
- ½ tsp. ground cayenne pepper
- 1 tsp. Minced fresh rosemary
- ¼ tsp. nutmeg
- 1 tsp. ground mustard seed
- 1 tsp. celery seed

Directions:

1. Set a small skillet over medium heat and grease it with canola oil.
2. Add garlic and sauté for 1 minute.
3. Mix cooked rice, sauteed garlic, ground chicken, and the rest of the ingredients in a bowl.
4. Stir well, cover, and refrigerate this chicken mixture for 1 hour.
5. Divide this chicken mixture into six equal parts and roll each into a sausage shape.
6. Place the sausages in a large, greased baking dish.
7. At 350°F, preheat your air fryer.

8. Air fry the chicken sausages for 10 minutes and flip them once cooked halfway through.
9. Serve.

Nutritional Facts: Calories 327; Fat 3.5g; Carbohydrate 41.9g; Protein 33g; Cholesterol 71mg; Sodium 62mg; Potassium 242mg

46. Balsamic Chicken Roast

Prep time: 20 mins

Cooking time: 1 hr.

Servings: 4

Ingredients:

- 1 (4 lbs.) whole chicken
- 1 tbsp. fresh rosemary
- 1 garlic clove, minced
- 1 tbsp. Olive oil
- ⅛ tsp. black pepper
- 8 sprigs of fresh rosemary
- ½ c. balsamic vinegar
- 1 tsp. brown sugar

Directions:

1. At 350°F, preheat your air fryer.
2. Mix garlic and rosemary and mince them together.
3. Loosen the chicken skin and rub its flesh with oil and herb mixture.
4. Place the chicken in a roasting dish and sprinkle black pepper on top.
5. Stuff the chicken cavity with rosemary spring and tie the legs of the chicken with kitchen twine.
6. Air fry the prepared chicken for 1 hour until tender.
7. Baste the chicken with pan juices after every 15-20 minutes.

8. Meanwhile, mix brown sugar and vinegar in a small saucepan and cook only until the sugar is dissolved.
9. Cut the chicken into smaller pieces and remove its skin,
10. Dip each piece in the vinegar sugar mixture and garnish with rosemary.
11. Serve.

Nutritional Facts: Calories 575; Fat 24.4g; Carbohydrate 1.9g; Protein 81.1g; Cholesterol 249mg; Sodium 243mg; Potassium 206mg

47. Chicken Piccata

Prep time: 15 mins

Cooking time: 48 mins

Servings: 4

Ingredients:

- 1 lb. baby new potatoes
- ½ c. low-fat parmesan grated
- 1 tsp. dried basil
- 1 tsp. dried oregano
- 1 lb. boneless chicken breast halves
- ½ c. cornmeal
- 1 tsp. lemon pepper
- 1 c. low-sodium chicken broth
- 1 tbsp. olive oil
- 2 tbsp. lemon juice
- 1 tbsp. unsalted butter

Directions:

1. At 400°F, preheat your air fryer.
2. Toss potatoes with herbs and oil in a baking dish and air fry them for 20 minutes.
3. Pound the chicken pieces into ¼ inch thickness with a mallet.
4. Coat the chicken with cornmeal and lemon pepper.

5. Air fry the chicken for 10-12 minutes in the air fryer and flip once cooked halfway through.
6. Transfer the chicken to a serving platter.
7. Add lemon juice, broth, and butter to a skillet.
8. Cook this mixture on a boil until reduced to half, then pour over the chicken.
9. Add potatoes to the chicken on the side and serve.

Nutritional Facts: Calories 497; Fat 10.2g; Carbohydrate 66.9g; Protein 36.1g; Cholesterol 83mg; Sodium 238mg; Potassium 301mg

48. Chicken Mushroom Ragu

Prep time: 15 mins

Cooking time: 28 mins

Servings: 4

Ingredients:

- 1 (28-oz.) can of no-salt-added whole peeled tomatoes
- ¼ c. olive oil
- 1 medium onion, chopped
- 2 medium carrots, chopped
- 8 oz. cremini mushrooms, quartered
- 1 ¾ lb. boneless, skinless chicken thighs
- 2 garlic cloves, grated
- ¼ c. tomato paste
- ½ c. dry red wine
- ¼ tsp. crushed red pepper
- 1 tbsp. fresh rosemary, chopped
- 1 lb. whole-wheat linguine
- ½ c. low-fat Romano cheese, grated
- ½ c. fresh parsley, chopped

Directions:

1. At 350°F, preheat your air fryer. Spread the chicken thighs in the air fryer basket. Air fry them for 15 minutes until tender. Cut the chicken into cubes.

2. Set a large pot on medium-high heat and add water to boil. Add pasta and cook until it is soft and al-dente, then drain.
3. Add tomatoes and their juice to a bowl and crush them with your hands. Add oil to an electric pressure cooker and heat it on Sauté mode. Add mushrooms, carrots, and onion, then sauté for 5 minutes.
4. Stir in tomato paste and garlic, then cook for 4 minutes. Add tomatoes, red pepper, and wine, then cook for 2 minutes.
5. Cover the pressure cooking lid and seal it. Cook the mixture for 2 minutes on high pressure.
6. Once done, release its pressure manually, then remove the lid. Add rosemary and diced chicken, then mix well.
7. Divide the pasta into the serving plates. Add the mushroom sauce, cheese, and parsley on top. Serve.

Nutritional Facts: Calories 524; Fat 20.2g; Carbohydrate 55.8g; Protein 28.1g; Cholesterol 127mg; Sodium 134mg; Potassium 755mg

49. Chicken Quesadillas

Prep time: 10 mins

Cooking time: 12 mins

Servings: 4

Ingredients:

- 4 boneless, skinless chicken breasts
- 1 c. onions, chopped
- ½ c. smoky salsa
- 1 c. fresh tomatoes, chopped
- 1 c. fresh cilantro, chopped
- 6 (8 inches) whole-wheat tortillas
- 1 c. reduced-fat cheddar cheese, shredded

Directions:

1. At 425°F, preheat your air fryer. Line the air fryer basket with parchment paper.
2. Cut the boneless chicken into cubes.
3. Add chicken and onions to the air fryer basket and cook for 5 minutes.
4. Remove the chicken from the basket and mix with cilantro, tomatoes, and salsa in a bowl.
5. Spread a tortilla on a working surface.
6. Rub its outer edges with water and add ½ C. of the chicken mixture on top while leaving ½ inch space around the rim.
7. Drizzle a tablespoon of cheese on the chicken mixture and fold the tortilla in half.
8. Press and seal the edges, then transfer this quesadilla to the air fryer basket
9. Spray cooking oil over the tortillas and air fry for 7 minutes.
10. Repeat the same steps with the remaining tortillas and filling.
11. Slice each in half and serve.

Nutritional Facts: Calories 488; Fat 21g; Carbohydrate 23.1g; Protein 50.9g; Cholesterol 154mg; Sodium 512mg; Potassium 301mg

50. Crusted Chicken

Prep time: 15 mins

Cooking time: 25 mins

Servings: 4

Ingredients:

- 8 saltine crackers, 2 inches square
- 1 tsp. paprika
- 2 boneless, skinless chicken breasts
- 4 tsp. honey

Directions:

1. At 350°F, preheat your air fryer.
2. Grease a large suitable baking dish with cooking spray.
3. Crush the crackers and mix them with paprika in a bowl.
4. Rub chicken with honey and coat it with the cracker mixture.
5. Place this chicken in the baking dish and air fry for 25 minutes.
6. Serve.

Nutritional Facts: Calories 241; Fat 7.5g; Carbohydrate 20.3g; Protein 22.2g; Cholesterol 62mg; Sodium 275mg; Potassium 217mg

51. Honey Dijon Chicken

Prep time: 15 mins

Cooking time: 10 mins

Servings: 4

Ingredients:

- 2 tbsp. olive oil
- 4 tbsp. Dijon mustard
- 4 tbsp. honey
- 3 tbsp. Mrs. Dash seasoning mix
- 4 (4 oz.) boneless chicken breasts

Directions:

1. At 350°F, preheat your air fryer.
2. Brush oil over the chicken and season it with honey, seasoning, and mustard.
3. Air fry the chicken for 10 minutes until golden brown; flip once cooked halfway through.
4. Serve warm.

Nutritional Facts: Calories 350; Fat 16g; Carbohydrate 18.1g; Protein 33.6g; Cholesterol 101mg; Sodium 276mg; Potassium 308mg

52. Garlic Herb Chicken

Prep time: 10 mins

Cooking time: 11 mins

Servings: 2

Ingredients:

- 2 tbsp. Mrs. Dash garlic and herb seasoning blend
- 1 lb. boneless, skinless chicken breasts
- 2 tsp. olive oil
- 1 tsp. Dijon-style mustard
- 2 tbsp. Lemon juice

Directions:

1. At 350°F, preheat your air fryer.
2. Grease it with olive oil and air fry the chicken for 10 minutes; flip once cooked halfway through.
3. Add mustard, lemon juice, and seasoning blend.
4. Air fry for 1 minute and serve warm.

Nutritional Facts: Calories 476; Fat 21.7g; Carbohydrate 0.5g; Protein 65.8g; Cholesterol 202mg; Sodium 226mg; Potassium 573mg

53. Onion Stuffed Whole Chicken

Prep time: 10 mins

Cooking time: 60 mins

Servings: 8

Ingredients:

- 1 (4-5 lb.) whole chicken
- 1 medium onion, peeled and quartered
- 1 tsp. Smoked paprika
- ½ tsp. Onion powder
- ½ tsp. Dried thyme
- ½ tsp. Garlic powder
- ¾ tsp. black pepper
- 2 tbsp. avocado oil

Directions:

1. Mix smoked paprika, onion powder, thyme, garlic powder, and black pepper in a bowl.
2. Stuff the whole chicken with onion quarters.
3. Place the whole chicken in a roasting pan and brush it with avocado oil
4. Rub the prepared mixture over the chicken liberally.
5. At 360°F, preheat your air fryer.
6. Place the whole stuffed chicken in the air fryer basket and air fry for 45 minutes.
7. Flip the chicken once cooked halfway through.
8. Cook the chicken for another 15 minutes.
9. Serve warm.

Nutritional Facts: Calories 444; Fat 17.3g; Carbohydrate 2g; Protein 65.9g; Cholesterol 202mg; Sodium 1068mg; Potassium 595mg

54. Crispy Air fried Chicken

Prep time: 10 mins

Cooking time: 14 mins

Servings: 2

Ingredients:

- 1.5 lbs. chicken thighs, boneless
- 1 c. cornflake crumbs
- ½ tsp. Italian herb seasoning
- ¼ tsp. Garlic powder
- ¼ tsp. onion powder
- 1 tsp. paprika
- Canola cooking spray

Directions:

1. At 350°F, preheat your air fryer.
2. Crush the cornflakes in a plastic bag with a rolling pin.
3. Mix the cornflakes crumbs with herb seasoning, garlic powder, onion powder, and paprika in a bowl.
4. Spray the chicken with cooking spray and coat it with the crumbs mixture.
5. Place the coated chicken in the air fryer basket and air fry for 14 minutes.
6. Serve warm.

Nutritional Facts: Calories 401; Fat 8.5g; Carbohydrate 42.5g; Protein 36.2g; Cholesterol 93mg; Sodium 92mg; Potassium 286mg

55. Sesame Chicken

Prep time: 10 mins

Cooking time: 8 mins

Servings: 2

Ingredients:

- 24 oz. boneless, skinless chicken breast, diced
- 2 garlic cloves diced
- 1½ tbsp. honey
- 1 tbsp. Low-sodium soy sauce
- ½ tsp. black pepper
- ¼ c. scallions diced
- 1 tsp. sesame seeds

Directions:

1. At 350°F, preheat your air fryer.
2. Mix garlic, black pepper, soy sauce, and honey in a large bowl.
3. Toss in chicken cubes and mix well.
4. Air fry the chicken for 8 minutes until tender and drizzle sesame seeds on top.
5. Serve warm.

Nutritional Facts: Calories 454; Fat 7.9g; Carbohydrate 30.8g; Protein 63.7g; Cholesterol 162mg; Sodium 230mg; Potassium 434mg

Chapter 6: Meat Recipes

56. Spicy Beef Kebabs

Prep time: 10 mins

Cooking time: 10 mins

Servings: 6

Ingredients:

- 2 yellow onions, chopped
- 2 tbsp. fresh lemon juice
- 2 c. fine-grind bulgur
- 1 ½ lb. lean ground beef
- ¼ c. chopped pine nuts
- 2 garlic cloves, minced
- 1 tsp. ground cumin
- ½ tsp. ground cinnamon
- ½ tsp. ground cardamom
- ½ tsp. black pepper
- 16 wooden skewers

For the Sauce:

- 2 c. fat-free plain yogurt
- ¼ c. tahini
- 2 tbsp. grated lemon zest
- 2 tsp. dry mustard
- 2 tbsp. chopped fresh cilantro

Directions:

1. Blend onion in a food processor until pureed, then strain through a fine sieve to get the juice.
2. Mix onion juice with lemon juice and enough water to make 1 ½ cup of liquid.
3. Add bulgur to this onion juice mixture and soak for 10 minutes.
4. Stir in black pepper, cardamom, cinnamon, cumin, garlic, pine nuts, and beef.
5. Mix this mixture well and take ⅓ cup of this mixture for each kebab, then shape each into a sausage shape.

6. Thread the beef sausages over the skewers.
7. Preheat your air fryer to 350°F and grease its grate with cooking spray.
8. Air fry the kebab for 10 minutes and flip them once cooked halfway through.
9. Meanwhile, mix yogurt, mustard, lemon zest, and tahini in a bowl.
10. Serve the kebabs with the yogurt dip.

Nutritional Facts: Calories 421; Fat 18.3g; Carbohydrate 23.7g; Protein 42.9g; Cholesterol 1mg; Sodium 63mg; Potassium 348mg

57. Pork Tenderloin With Balsamic Sauce

Prep time: 15 minutes

Cooking time: 25 mins

Servings: 2

Ingredients:

- 1 tbsp. olive oil
- 1 lb. lean pork tenderloin, trimmed
- Black pepper, to taste
- 2 c. chopped onion
- 2 c. chopped apple
- 1 ½ tbsp. fresh rosemary, chopped
- 1 c. low-sodium chicken broth
- 1 ½ tbsp. balsamic vinegar

Directions:

1. At 450°F, preheat your air fryer.
2. Grease a baking pan with cooking spray.
3. Rub the pork with oil and black pepper.
4. Air fry the pork for 15 minutes in the preheated air fryer.
5. Meanwhile, sauté apple, onion, and rosemary in a skillet for 5 minutes.
6. Stir in vinegar and broth, then cook for 5 minutes.
7. Slice the pork and serve with apple sauce.

Nutritional Facts: Calories 565; Fat 15.9g; Carbohydrate 43.8g; Protein 62.4g; Cholesterol 166mg; Sodium 173mg; Potassium 1394mg

58. Pork With Herbes De Provence

Prep time: 10 mins

Cooking time: 6 mins

Servings: 2

Ingredients:

- 8 oz. lean pork tenderloin, crosswise into 6 pieces
- Black pepper, to taste
- ½ tsp. Herbes de Provence
- ¼ c. dry white wine

Directions:

1. Rub the pork pieces with black pepper.
2. Place the pork between two parchment papers and pound it with a mallet.
3. At 350°F, preheat your air fryer.
4. Air fry the pork pieces for 6 minutes.
5. Drizzle the wine and Herbes de Provence over the pork.
6. Slice and serve.

Nutritional Facts: Calories 312; Fat 14.2g; Carbohydrate 1.8g; Protein 37.3g; Cholesterol 83mg; Sodium 166mg; Potassium 507mg

59. Pork Chops With Black Currant Sauce

Prep time: 10 mins

Cooking time: 12 mins

Servings: 6

Ingredients:

- ¼ c. black currant jam
- 2 tbsp. Dijon mustard
- 2 tsp. olive oil
- 6 (4-oz.) lean pork loin chops, trimmed fat
- ⅓ c. wine vinegar
- ⅛ tsp. black pepper

Directions:

1. Mix black currant jam with mustard in a bowl.
2. At 350°F, preheat your air fryer.
3. Brush the pork with oil and air fry for 10 minutes.
4. Add the jam-mustard mixture on top and air fry for 2 minutes.
5. Garnish with black pepper and vinegar.
6. Serve.

Nutritional Facts: Calories 429; Fat 32.5g; Carbohydrate 6.9g; Protein 27.7g; Cholesterol 103mg; Sodium 189mg; Potassium 503mg

60. Pork Fajitas

Prep time: 15 mins

Cooking time: 18 mins

Servings: 8

Ingredients:

- 1 tsp. Ground cumin
- ½ tsp. Oregano
- ½ tsp. Paprika
- ¼ tsp. Ground coriander
- ¼ tsp. garlic powder
- 1 lb. lean pork tenderloin, cut into strips
- 1 small onion, peeled
- 8 whole-wheat flour tortillas, 8 inches
- 3 green bell pepper
- 3 yellow bell pepper

Directions:

1. Preheat your air fryer to 350°F.
2. Mix garlic powder, coriander, paprika, oregano, and cumin.
3. Coat the pork strips with the spice mixture.
4. Air fry the pork strips for 8 minutes until tender.
5. Air fry the onion and bell pepper for 10 minutes until soft.
6. Cut the onion and bell peppers into strips.
7. Divide the pork, bell pepper, and onion over the tortillas.
8. Roll the tortillas and serve.

Nutritional Facts: Calories 279; Fat 6.4g; Carbohydrate 34.1g; Protein 22.2g; Cholesterol 46mg; Sodium 390mg; Potassium 581mg

61. Spiced Pork Medallions

Prep time: 10 mins

Cooking time: 30 mins

Servings: 2

Ingredients:

- 2 tbsp. low-sodium soy sauce
- 1 tbsp. green onion, chopped
- 3 garlic cloves, minced
- 1 tbsp. Olive oil
- ¾ tsp. five-spice powder
- 1 lb. lean pork tenderloin, fat trimmed
- 1 tbsp. olive oil
- ½ c. water
- ¼ c. dry white wine
- ⅓ c. chopped yellow onion
- ½ head green cabbage, sliced

Directions:

1. Mix five-spice powder, olive oil, garlic, green onion, and soy sauce in a bowl.
2. Add pork to the marinade, cover, and marinate, then refrigerate for 2 hours.
3. At 400°F, preheat your air fryer.
4. Rub the pork with oil and air fry for 20-25 minutes.
5. Transfer the cooked pork to a plate and keep it aside.
6. Add wine to the same pan and place it over medium-high heat.
7. Deglaze the pan and stir in onion, then cook for 1 minute.
8. Add cabbage and one tablespoon of water, then cook for 4 minutes.
9. Slice pork and serve with cabbage mixture on the side.

Nutritional Facts: Calories 496; Fat 15.2g; Carbohydrate 17.6g; Protein 64.4g; Cholesterol 166mg; Sodium 349mg; Potassium 1334mg

62. Curried Pork Tenderloin

Prep time: 10 mins

Cooking time: 22 mins

Servings: 4

Ingredients:

- 16 oz. lean pork tenderloin, cut into 4 pieces
- 1 ½ Tbsp. curry powder
- 1 tbsp. olive oil
- 2 medium yellow onions, chopped
- 2 c. apple cider
- 1 tart apple, peeled, chopped
- 1 tbsp. cornstarch

Directions:

1. Rub the pork tenderloin with curry powder and oil, then keep it aside for 15 minutes.
2. At 400°F, preheat your air fryer.
3. Air fry the marinated pork for 10 minutes.
4. Transfer the cooked pork to a plate and keep it aside.
5. Sauté onion in the same skillet for 5 minutes until golden brown.
6. Add 1 ½ cup of cider and cook until reduced to half.
7. Stir in the remaining cider, cornstarch, and apple, then cook for 2 minutes until it thickens.
8. Return the pork to the skillet and cook for 5 minutes on a simmer.
9. Slice the pork and serve with its sauce.

Nutritional Facts: Calories 317; Fat 8.1g; Carbohydrate 30.5g; Protein 30.8g; Cholesterol 83mg; Sodium 72mg; Potassium 801mg

63. Beef Stew With Fennel

Prep time: 20 mins

Cooking time: 69 mins

Servings: 8

Ingredients:

- 3 tbsp. all-purpose flour
- 1 lb. boneless lean beef stew meat, diced
- 2 tbsp. olive oil
- ½ fennel bulb, trimmed and sliced
- 3 large shallots, chopped
- ¾ tsp. black pepper, divided
- 2 fresh thyme sprigs
- 1 bay leaf
- 3 c. no-salt vegetable stock
- ½ c. red wine
- 4 large carrots, peeled and diced
- 4 large red-skinned potatoes, peeled and diced
- 18 small boiling onions, halved crosswise
- 3 portobello mushrooms, diced
- ⅓ c. chopped fresh flat-leaf parsley

Directions:

1. Spread flour on a plate and coat the beef cubes with the flour.
2. At 350°F, preheat your air fryer and grease it with oil.
3. Air fry the coated beef for 30 minutes, flip it once cooked halfway through, then transfer to a plate.
4. Add shallots and fennel to a greased oil pan and cook for 8 minutes.
5. Stir in bay leaf, thyme sprigs, and ¼ teaspoon of black pepper and cook for 1 minute.

6. Add the air-fried beef to the same pan and add wine and vegetable stock.
7. Cook the beef stew for 10 minutes.
8. Stir in mushrooms, onion, potatoes, and carrots, then cook for 30 minutes.
9. Discard the bay leaf and thyme sprigs.
10. Garnish with one teaspoon of pepper and parsley.
11. Serve.

Nutritional Facts: Calories 456; Fat 21.3g; Carbohydrate 22.6g; Protein 43.2g; Cholesterol 117mg; Sodium 179mg; Potassium 435mg

64. Beef Brisket Stew

Prep time: 15 mins

Cooking time: 1 hour 6 mins.

Servings: 6

Ingredients:

- 1 tbsp. olive oil
- 2 ½ lbs. lean beef brisket, cut into cubes
- Black pepper, to taste
- 1 ½ c. onions, chopped
- 4 garlic cloves, smashed and peeled
- 1 tsp. dried thyme
- 1 can (14.5 oz.) of no-salt-added tomatoes and liquid
- ¼ c. red wine vinegar
- 1 c. low-sodium beef stock

Directions:

1. At 350°F, preheat your air fryer.
2. Rub one tablespoon of oil over the brisket while seasoning it with black pepper.
3. Air fry the brisket for 30 minutes.
4. Add onions to the Dutch oven, then cook for 5 minutes.
5. Stir in thyme and garlic, then cook for 1 minute.
6. Add tomatoes, beef, vinegar, and stock, then cover and cook for 30 minutes.
7. Serve warm.

Nutritional Facts: Calories 428; Fat 14.2g; Carbohydrate 6.3g; Protein 58.2g; Cholesterol 169mg; Sodium 133mg; Potassium 952mg

65. Beef Barley Stew

Prep time: 10 mins

Cooking time: 39 mins

Servings: 4

Ingredients:

- 1 lb. lean beef round steak
- 2 tsp. canola oil
- 2 c. yellow onions, diced
- 1 c. celery, diced
- 1 c. Roma tomatoes, diced
- ½ c. sweet potato, diced
- ½ c. white potato with skin, diced
- ½ c. mushrooms, diced
- 1 c. carrot, sliced
- 4 garlic cloves, chopped
- 1 c. kale, chopped
- ¼ c. uncooked barley
- ¼ c. red wine vinegar
- 1 tsp. balsamic vinegar
- 3 c. low-sodium vegetable stock
- 1 tsp. dried sage, crushed
- 1 tsp. minced fresh thyme
- 1 tbsp. minced fresh parsley
- 1 tbsp. dried oregano
- 1 tsp. dried rosemary, minced
- Black pepper, to taste

Directions:

1. At 350°F, preheat your air fryer.
2. Set a grill grate in the air fryer basket.
3. Air fry the round steak for 14 minutes, then cut it into cubes.
4. Set a large stockpot over medium-high heat.
5. Grease it with oil and add vegetables, then cook for 10 minutes.
6. Stir in barley, then cook for 5 minutes.
7. Pat dry the steak with a paper towel and cut it into half-inch pieces.
8. Add the steak, spices, herbs, stock, and vinegar to the pot.
9. Cook this stew to a boil, cover, and cook for 10 minutes on a simmer.
10. Serve warm.

Nutritional Facts: Calories 471; Fat 13.3g; Carbohydrate 44.4g; Protein 42.5g; Cholesterol 95mg; Sodium 168mg; Potassium 1587mg

66. Beef Vegetable Kebabs

Prep time: 30 mins

Cooking time: 10 mins

Servings: 2

Ingredients:

- 4 oz. beef top sirloin, diced
- 1 tbsp. fat-free Italian dressing
- 1 green bell pepper, seeded and cut into squares
- 1 yellow bell pepper, cut into squares
- 1 small onion, cut into 4 wedges
- 2 wooden skewers

Directions:

1. Mix beef pieces with Italian dressing in a bowl.
2. Cover and refrigerate this beef for 20 minutes.
3. Preheat your air fryer to 360°F and grease it with cooking spray.
4. Thread the beef cubes, green and yellow bell pepper, and onion pieces on the skewers alternately.
5. Air fry the skewers for 10 minutes and flip them once cooked halfway through.
6. Serve warm.

Nutritional Facts: Calories 353; Fat 5.5g; Carbohydrate 52.7g; Protein 23.9g; Cholesterol 51mg; Sodium 169mg; Potassium 1106mg

67. Asian Pork Tenderloin

Prep time: 10 mins

Cooking time: 15 mins

Servings: 2

Ingredients:

- 2 tbsp. sesame seeds
- 1 tsp. Ground coriander
- ⅛ tsp. Cayenne pepper
- ⅛ tsp. Celery seed
- ½ tsp. Minced onion
- ¼ tsp. Ground cumin
- ⅛ tsp. ground cinnamon
- 1 tbsp. sesame oil
- 1 lb. lean pork tenderloin, sliced into 4 portions

Directions:

1. At 350°F, preheat your air fryer.
2. Grease a baking dish with cooking spray.
3. Toast the sesame seeds in a suitable frying pan for 2 minutes, then transfer them to a bowl.
4. Stir in sesame oil, cinnamon, cumin, onion, celery seed, cayenne pepper, and coriander.
5. Place the pork in the prepared baking dish and rub the prepared mixture over the pork.
6. Air fry the pork for 15 minutes until tender.
7. Serve.

Nutritional Facts: Calories 439; Fat 19.3g; Carbohydrate 2.5g; Protein 61.1g; Cholesterol 166mg; Sodium 131mg; Potassium 1008mg

68.   New York Strip Steak

Prep time: 10 mins

Cooking time: 22 mins

Servings: 2

Ingredients:

- 2 New York strip steaks
- 1 tsp. trans-free margarine
- 3 garlic cloves, chopped
- ¼ tsp. thyme
- ¼ tsp. rosemary
- ¼ c. whiskey

Directions:

1. At 350°F, preheat your air fryer.
2. Air fry the steaks for 20 minutes and flip once cooked halfway through.
3. Sauté garlic with margarine in a skillet for 1 minute.
4. Stir in rosemary, whiskey, and thyme, then cook for 1 minute.
5. Place the steaks in the skillet and coat them with a whiskey mixture.
6. Serve warm.

Nutritional Facts: Calories 393; Fat 20.1g; Carbohydrate 2.2g; Protein 42.6g; Cholesterol 112mg; Sodium 123mg; Potassium 630mg

69. Shepherd's Pie

Prep time: 10 mins

Cooking time: 1 hr. 15 mins

Servings: 4

Ingredients:

- 1 head of cauliflower, cut into florets
- 1 garlic clove, peeled
- 1 leek, white only, quartered
- 1 tbsp. trans-free margarine
- Black pepper, to taste
- 2 c. cooked chopped turkey breast
- 1 tbsp. olive oil
- 1 c. carrots, diced
- 1 c. celery, diced
- 2 c. onion, diced
- 1 tsp. dried thyme
- 3 tsp. sliced garlic
- 8 oz. can low-sodium tomato sauce
- 1 tsp. orange zest
- 2 tsp. balsamic vinegar
- 1 c. red wine

Directions:

1. At 350°F, preheat your air fryer.
2. Add cauliflower, leeks, and garlic to a steamer basket.
3. Boil water in a steamer and place the basket into it.
4. Cover and steam the veggies for 30 minutes.
5. Puree these veggies in a blender until smooth.

6. Stir in black pepper and margarine.
7. Sauté garlic, thyme, onions, celery, and carrots with oil in a skillet for 6 minutes.
8. Stir in turkey and cook for 3 minutes.
9. Add red wine and cook until it's reduced to half.
10. Stir in tomato sauce, vinegar, and black pepper.
11. Spread this filling in a suitable casserole dish and top it with a mashed cauliflower mixture.
12. Air fry the shepherd's pie for 30 minutes in the preheated air fryer.
13. Serve warm.

Nutritional Facts: Calories 248; Fat 7g; Carbohydrate 23.4g; Protein 14.3g; Cholesterol 27mg; Sodium 233mg; Potassium 924mg

70. Pork Tenderloin With Fennel Sauce

Prep time: 10 mins

Cooking time: 24 mins

Servings: 6

Ingredients:

- 4 lean pork tenderloin fillets
- 2 tbsp. olive oil
- 1 tsp. fennel seeds
- 1 fennel bulb, cored and sliced
- 1 sweet onion, sliced
- ½ c. dry white wine
- 1 can (12 oz.) of low-sodium chicken broth
- Fennel fronds, for garnish
- Orange slices, for garnish

Directions:

1. Place the pork fillets between two wax papers and pound them with a mallet.

2. Sauté fennel seeds with oil in a skillet for 3 minutes.
3. At 350°F, preheat your air fryer.
4. Rub the pork with oil and fennel seeds, then cook for 6 minutes.
5. Add onion and fennel to the same skillet and sauté for 5 minutes.
6. Add chicken broth and wine, then cook until it is reduced to half.
7. Stir in pork, cover, and cook on low heat for 5 minutes.
8. Serve warm.

Nutritional Facts: Calories 407; Fat 16.8g; Carbohydrate 7.3g; Protein 50.8g; Cholesterol 150mg; Sodium 272mg; Potassium 213mg

Chapter 7: Fish and Seafood Recipes

71. Chipotle Spiced Shrimp

Prep time: 10 mins

Cooking time: 5 mins

Servings: 2

Ingredients:

- 1 lb. uncooked shrimp, peeled and deveined
- 2 tbsp. low-sodium tomato paste
- 1 ½ tsp. Water
- ½ tsp. Olive oil
- ½ tsp. Minced garlic
- ½ tsp. Chipotle chili powder
- ½ tsp. chopped fresh oregano

Directions:

1. Mix tomato paste, oil, water, chili powder, oregano, and garlic.
2. Toss in shrimp, mix well to coat, cover and refrigerate for 5 minutes.
3. At 300°F, preheat your air fryer and grease it with cooking spray.
4. Air fry the shrimp for 5 minutes.
5. Serve.

Nutritional Facts: Calories 295; Fat 5.1g; Carbohydrate 6.9g; Protein 52.4g; Cholesterol 478mg; Sodium 269mg; Potassium 556mg

72. Air fried Cod Pocket

Prep time: 10 mins

Cooking time: 10 mins

Servings: 4

Ingredients:

- 1 carrot, cut into strips
- 1 onion, cut into strips
- 4 cod fillets, 4 oz.
- 2 tbsp. honey
- 4 tsp. black pepper
- 4 tsp. parsley, chopped
- 1 tsp. lemon zest
- Cooking spray

Directions:

1. At 325°F, preheat your air fryer.
2. Take 4 (6 inches) squares of aluminum sheet and fold the edge of each square to make the pockets.
3. Divide the carrot and onion into the pockets and set one cod fillet each.
4. Spray the cooking spray over the cod.
5. Drizzle black pepper, parsley, and lemon zest on top of the cod.
6. Place the pockets in the air fryer basket.
7. Air fry the cod for 10 minutes in the preheated air fryer.
8. Serve warm.

Nutritional Facts: Calories 146; Fat 1.2g; Carbohydrate 13.2g; Protein 20.8g; Cholesterol 55mg; Sodium 129mg; Potassium 5mg

73. Halibut With Tomato Relish

Prep time: 10 mins

Cooking time: 15 mins

Servings: 4

Ingredients:

- 2 tomatoes, chopped
- 2 tbsp. fresh basil, chopped
- 1 tsp. fresh oregano, chopped
- 1 tbsp. minced garlic
- 2 tsp. olive oil
- 4 halibut fillets

Directions:

1. At 350°F, preheat your air fryer.
2. Grease a suitable baking pan with cooking spray.
3. Mix tomato, garlic, oregano, basil, and olive oil in a bowl.
4. Place the halibut fillets in the baking pan and spread half over the tomato mixture on top.
5. Air fry the fillets for 15 minutes and cut them into 2-3 smaller pieces.
6. Garnish with remaining relish.
7. Serve.

Nutritional Facts: Calories 354; Fat 9.2g; Carbohydrate 3.4g; Protein 61.3g; Cholesterol 93mg; Sodium 159mg; Potassium 1471mg

74. Crusted Snapper Curry

Prep time: 10 mins

Cooking time: 15 mins

Servings: 4

Ingredients:

- ½ tsp. coconut extract
- 1 c. low-fat soy milk
- 1 tsp. Cornstarch
- ½ tsp. fennel seed
- 1 tbsp. turmeric
- 1 tsp. ground coriander
- 1 tsp. ground cumin
- 1 tsp. paprika
- 1 tsp. canola oil
- 2 tbsp. minced ginger
- 2 garlic cloves, minced
- 1 c. onion, sliced
- 1 c. red bell pepper, sliced
- 1 poblano pepper, sliced
- 2 c. celery, sliced
- 2 c. bok choy, sliced
- 4 6 oz. red snapper fillets
- 1 c. breadcrumbs
- ½ c. fat-free milk
- Black pepper to taste

Directions:

1. At 350°F, preheat your air fryer.
2. Dip the snapper in the milk, then coat with the breadcrumbs.

3. Air fry these fillets for 10 minutes and flip them once cooked halfway through.
4. Mix spices, cornstarch, soy milk, and coconut extract in a small bowl.
5. Set a large suitable skillet over medium-high heat and grease it with oil.
6. Add bok choy, celery, peppers, onion, garlic, and ginger, then cook for 5 minutes.
7. Stir in spice-milk mixture, then cook to a simmer and remove from the heat.
8. Add the air-fried fish and flip to coat with the gravy.
9. Serve warm.

Nutritional Facts: Calories 430; Fat 35.1g; Carbohydrate 41g; Protein 15.4g; Cholesterol 0mg; Sodium 366mg; Potassium 541mg

75. Grouper With Tomato Sauce

Prep time: 10 mins

Cooking time: 29 mins

Servings: 4

Ingredients:

- 4 grouper fillets
- ¼ tsp. black pepper, divided
- 1 ½ tbsp. olive oil
- 1 yellow onion, chopped
- 2 cloves of garlic, minced
- 1 c. low-sodium tomato paste
- 2 tbsp. fresh lime juice

Directions:

1. Season the grouper steaks with ⅛ teaspoon of black pepper.
2. At 350°F, preheat your air fryer. Grease it with 1 ½ teaspoon of olive oil and air fry the fish for 2 minutes per side.
3. Transfer the fish to a plate and keep it aside.
4. Add remaining oil to the pan and add onion.
5. Sauté for 6 minutes, then stir in garlic.
6. Sauté for 1 minute, stir in tomato paste, and then cook for 10 minutes on a simmer.
7. Add the remaining ⅛ teaspoon of black pepper, then add the fish to the pan.
8. Cover and cook on a simmer for 8 minutes.

9. Add lime juice and serve warm.

Nutritional Facts: Calories 368; Fat 9.6g; Carbohydrate 16g; Protein 53g; Cholesterol 95mg; Sodium 377mg; Potassium 1347mg

76. Grilled Salmon With Maple Glaze

Prep time: 10 mins

Cooking time: 12 mins

Servings: 4

Ingredients:

- ¼ c. maple syrup
- 1 garlic clove, minced
- ¼ c. balsamic vinegar
- 2 lbs. salmon, cut into 6 equal-sized fillets
- ⅛ tsp. cracked black pepper

Directions:

1. At 450°F, preheat your air fryer.
2. Set a small saucepan over low heat and add balsamic vinegar, garlic, and maple syrup.
3. Cook this mixture for 2 minutes, then transfer to a bowl.
4. Pat dry the salmon and place it in the air fryer basket with a grill grate.
5. Brush the vinegar mixture over the salmon.
6. Air fry the salmon in the preheated air fryer for 5 minutes and flip the salmon.
7. Continue to air fry for another 5 minutes.
8. Drizzle black pepper on top.
9. Serve warm.

Nutritional Facts: Calories 356; Fat 14g; Carbohydrate 13.7g; Protein 44.1g; Cholesterol 100mg; Sodium 103mg; Potassium 926mg

77. Roasted Salmon

Prep time: 10 mins

Cooking time: 12 mins

Servings: 2

Ingredients:

- 2 5-oz. pieces of salmon with skin
- 2 tsp. Extra-virgin olive oil
- ½ tbsp. black pepper
- 1 tbsp. lemon juice
- 1 tbsp. fresh tarragon leaves

Directions:

1. At 425°F, preheat your air fryer.
2. Place the salmon in the air fryer basket and brush the oil, black pepper, and lemon juice on top.
3. Add tarragon leaves on top and air fry for 12 minutes.
4. Flip the salmon once cooked halfway through.
5. Discard the tarragon leaves.
6. Serve the fish with your favorite salad.

Nutritional Facts: Calories 143; Fat 5.8g; Carbohydrate 0.5g; Protein 21.3g; Cholesterol 55mg; Sodium 96mg; Potassium 32mg

78.   Shrimp Kebabs

Prep time: 10 mins

Cooking time: 4 mins

Servings: 4

Ingredients:

- 2 wooden skewers
- 1 lemon, juiced
- 1 Tbsp. olive oil
- 2 tsp. garlic, minced
- 1 tsp. fresh tarragon, chopped
- 1 tsp. Fresh rosemary, chopped
- ¼ tsp. black pepper
- 12 pieces of shrimp, peeled and deveined

Directions:

1. At 300°F, preheat your air fryer.
2. Mix seasonings, herbs, garlic, lemon juice, and olive oil in a bowl.
3. Toss in shrimp, then mix well to coat.
4. Thread the shrimp on the skewers.
5. Air fry the shrimp skewers for 4 minutes and flip them once cooked halfway through.
6. Serve.

Nutritional Facts: Calories 112; Fat 4.7g; Carbohydrate 1.8g; Protein 15.2g; Cholesterol 139mg; Sodium 162mg; Potassium 126mg

79. Air Fried Sole

Prep time: 10 mins

Cooking time: 10 mins

Servings: 2

Ingredients:

- 1 tsp. olive oil
- Black pepper, to taste
- 2 sole (flounder) fillets, each 5 oz.
- ½ tsp. almond butter, melted
- 1 tsp. parsley, chopped

Directions:

1. At 400°F, preheat your air fryer.
2. Grease a baking dish with olive oil.
3. Place the sole fish in the dish and brush it with butter.
4. Drizzle black pepper on top and air fry for 10 minutes.
5. Garnish with parsley and serve warm.

Nutritional Facts: Calories 101; Fat 2.8g; Carbohydrate 2.1g; Protein 12.1g; Cholesterol 75mg; Sodium 244mg; Potassium 179mg

80. Air Fried Swordfish

Prep time: 10 mins

Cooking time: 13 mins

Servings: 4

Ingredients:

- 4 swordfish fillets
- 1 tbsp. black pepper
- ½ tsp. canola oil
- ½ tsp. garlic, chopped
- ½ red bell pepper, chopped
- ½ yellow bell pepper, chopped
- ½ green bell pepper, chopped
- 1 tbsp. lemon juice

Directions:

1. At 375°F, preheat your air fryer.
2. Layer a baking dish with parchment paper.
3. Place the swordfish in the baking dish and drizzle black pepper on top.
4. Air fry the fish for 10 minutes in the preheated air fryer.
5. Meanwhile, sauté garlic with oil in a skillet for 30 seconds.
6. Stir in bell peppers, lemon juice, and parsley, then cook for 2 minutes.
7. Serve the fish with the pepper mixture on top.

Nutritional Facts: Calories 183; Fat 6.1g; Carbohydrate 3.4g; Protein 27g; Cholesterol 53mg; Sodium 241mg; Potassium 413mg

Chapter 8: Vegetarian Recipes

81. Marinated Mushrooms

Prep time: 10 mins

Cooking time: 7 mins

Servings: 2

Ingredients:

- 1 lb. button mushrooms, stemmed
- ½ c. balsamic vinegar
- 1 tbsp. Brown sugar
- ¼ tsp. dried rosemary
- 1 tsp. minced garlic
- 2 tbsp, green onion, chopped

Directions:

1. Mix vinegar, brown sugar, rosemary, and garlic in a bowl.
2. Stir in mushrooms, mix well and leave for 10 minutes.
3. Spread the mushrooms in the air fryer basket and air fry for 7 minutes.
4. Garnish with green onion.
5. Enjoy.

Nutritional Facts: Calories 220; Fat 2.8g; Carbohydrate 17.8g; Protein 14.6g; Cholesterol 23mg; Sodium 298mg; Potassium 759mg

82. Barley Risotto

Prep time: 15 mins

Cooking time: 1 hr. 20 mins

Servings: 6

Ingredients:

- 10 large plum (Roma) tomatoes, quartered
- 2 tbsp. olive oil
- ½ tsp. black pepper, divided
- 4 c. low-sodium vegetable stock
- 3 c. water
- 2 shallots, chopped
- ¼ c. dry white wine
- 2 c. pearl barley
- 3 tbsp. fresh basil, chopped
- 3 tbsp. fresh flat-leaf parsley, chopped
- 1 ½ tbsp. fresh thyme, chopped
- ½ c. grated low-fat Parmesan cheese
- ¼ c. croutons

Directions:

1. At 450°F, preheat your air fryer.
2. Spread the tomatoes in the air fryer basket and drizzle one tablespoon of olive oil and ¼ teaspoon of black pepper.
3. Air fry the tomatoes for 20 minutes.
4. Add vegetable stock and water to a saucepan and cook to a boil.
5. Sauté shallots with one tablespoon of oil in a pan for 3 minutes.
6. Stir in white wine and cook for 1 minute.
7. Add barley and cook for 1 minute, then transfer to the stock mixture.
8. Cook the barley soup for 50 minutes, add tomatoes, and cook for 5 minutes.
9. Garnish with croutons, parsley, thyme, and cheese.
10. Serve warm.

Nutritional Facts: Calories 272; Fat 4.7g; Carbohydrate 51.7g; Protein 8.2g; Cholesterol 0mg; Sodium 199mg; Potassium 629mg

83. Black Bean Wrap

Prep time: 15 mins

Cooking time: 5 mins

Servings: 6

Ingredients:

- 1 ½ c. canned low-sodium black beans, drained
- 1 ½ c. frozen corn kernels, thawed
- 3 tbsp. fresh cilantro, chopped
- 2 tbsp. chopped green chili peppers
- 4 green onions, diced
- 1 tomato, diced
- 1 tbsp. garlic, chopped
- 6 whole-grain tortilla wraps
- ¾ c. low-fat shredded cheddar cheese

Directions:

1. Mix garlic, tomato, onions, chili peppers, cilantro, corn, and black beans in a microwave-safe bowl.
2. Cook the beans mixture in the microwave for 2 minutes.
3. Place the tortillas on the working surface and divide the black bean mixture on top of the tortillas.
4. Divide the beans and cheese on top of the tortillas.
5. Spread the filling and fold the tortillas in half. Place them on a plate.
6. At 350°F, preheat your air fryer.
7. Place the wraps in the air fryer and air fry for 5 minutes.

Nutritional Facts: Calories 324; Fat 8.8g; Carbohydrate 48.8g; Protein 14.3g; Cholesterol 15mg; Sodium 330mg; Potassium 397mg

84. Vegetable Kebabs

Prep time: 15 mins

Cooking time: 10 mins

Servings: 2

Ingredients:

- 2 bell peppers, diced
- 1 eggplant, diced
- 1 zucchini, diced
- ½ onion, diced
- Black pepper, to taste

Directions:

1. At 390°F, preheat your Air fryer.
2. Thread bell peppers, eggplant, zucchini, and onion on wooden skewers, alternately.
3. Spread the skewers in the Air fryer basket.
4. Spray them with cooking spray and season with black pepper.
5. Return the Air fryer basket to the Air fryer.
6. Air fry these skewers for 10 minutes. Serve warm.

Nutritional Facts: Calories 439; Fat 15.7g; Carbohydrate 72.6g; Protein 9.2g; Cholesterol 0mg; Sodium 154mg; Potassium 756mg

85. Buffalo Cauliflower

Prep time: 10 mins

Cooking time: 10 mins.

Servings: 4

Ingredients:

- 1 large cauliflower head, cut into steaks
- Black pepper, to taste

For the Dry Mixture:

- 1 ½ c. almond flour
- ⅓ c. xanthan gum
- 1 tbsp. garlic powder
- 1 tbsp. onion powder
- 1 tbsp. paprika
- 2 tsp. cayenne

For the Wet Mixture:

- 1 c. soymilk
- 2 tsp. apple cider vinegar
- 2 tbsp. vegan egg powder
- ½ c. ice-cold water
- 2 tbsp. bourbon
- 1 tbsp. hot sauce

Directions:

1. Mix soy milk with all the wet and dry ingredients in a bowl.
2. Dip the cauliflower in the flour batter
3. At 400°F, preheat your Air fryer.
4. Spread the cauliflower in the Air fryer basket.
5. Return the Air fryer basket to the Air fryer.
6. Air fry the cauliflower for 10 minutes.

7. Shake them once cooked halfway through. Serve.

Nutritional Facts: Calories 159; Fat 0.8g; Carbohydrate 30.7g; Protein 9.5g; Cholesterol 0mg; Sodium 31mg; Potassium 719mg

86. Sumac Roasted Cauliflower

Prep time: 10 mins

Cooking time: 13 mins

Servings: 2

Ingredients:

- 4 c. medium-sized cauliflower florets
- 1 tsp. canola oil
- A pinch of salt
- 2 tsp. Lemon juice
- ⅛ tsp. sumac

Directions:

1. At 400°F, preheat your Air fryer.
2. Toss cauliflower with lemon and the rest of the ingredients in a bowl.
3. Spread the cauliflower in the Air fryer basket.
4. Return the Air fryer basket to the Air fryer.
5. Air fry the cauliflower for 13 minutes.
6. Shake them once cooked halfway through. Serve

Nutritional Facts: Calories 400; Fat 5g; Carbohydrate 72.3g; Protein 18.3g; Cholesterol 1mg; Sodium 289mg; Potassium 418m

87. Sesame-Crusted Tofu

Prep time: 10 mins

Cooking time: 6 mins

Servings: 2

Ingredients:

- 1 lb. firm tofu, drained
- ¼ c. fat-free milk
- 2 egg whites, beaten
- ¼ tsp. black pepper
- 1 c. plain flour
- 2 tbsp. white sesame seeds
- ½ tsp. sesame oil

Directions:

1. Mix milk with black pepper, egg whites, and milk in a bowl.
2. Spread flour on a plate.
3. Dip the tofu cubes in the milk mixture, then coat with flour.
4. At 350°F, preheat your air fryer.
5. Spread the tofu cubes in the air fryer and air fry for 6 minutes.
6. Garnish with sesame seeds.
7. Enjoy.

Nutritional Facts: Calories 320; Fat 11.2g; Carbohydrate 38.5g; Protein 16.6g; Cholesterol 2mg; Sodium 151mg; Potassium 274mg

88. Stuffed Eggplant

Prep time: 15 mins

Cooking time: 30 mins

Servings: 2

Ingredients:

- 1 medium eggplant
- 1 c. water
- 1 tbsp. olive oil
- 6 oz. boneless chicken breast, chopped
- ¼ c. onion, chopped
- ½ c. bell peppers, chopped
- 1 c. canned unsalted tomatoes, drained
- ¼ c. tomato liquid
- ¼ c. celery, chopped
- 1 c. fresh mushrooms, sliced
- ¾ c. quinoa, cooked
- Black pepper, to taste
- Cilantro, to garnish

Directions:

1. At 350°F, preheat your air fryer.
2. Grease a baking dish with cooking spray.
3. Cut the eggplant in half lengthwise and scoop out the flesh from the center to get ¼ inch thick shells.
4. Place the eggplant shells in a baking dish and add a splash of water to the bottom of the dish.
5. Chop the scooped-out eggplant into cubes.
6. Sauté chickens strips with oil in a large skillet for 5 minutes.
7. Stir in peppers, tomatoes, tomato juice, mushrooms, celery, onion, and eggplant cubes, then cook for 10 minutes.
8. Divide the filling into the eggplant shells and drizzle quinoa and black pepper on top of the stuffed eggplants.
9. Air fry them for 15 minutes.

10. Garnish with cilantro.
11. Serve warm.

Nutritional Facts: Calories 350; Fat 12g; Carbohydrate 42.9g; Protein 26.7g; Cholesterol 54mg; Sodium 148mg; Potassium 1969mg

89. Vegetable Calzone

Prep time: 15 mins

Cooking time: 15 mins

Servings: 4

Ingredients:

- 3 asparagus stalks, cut into 1-inch pieces
- ½ c. spinach, chopped
- ½ c. broccoli, chopped
- ½ c. mushrooms, sliced
- 2 tbsp. garlic, minced
- 2 tsp. olive oil
- ½ lb. pizza dough, thawed
- 1 medium tomato, sliced
- ½ c. low-fat shredded part-skim mozzarella

Directions:

1. At 400°F, preheat your air fryer.
2. Sauté mushrooms, broccoli, spinach, asparagus, and garlic with one teaspoon in a skillet for 5 minutes.
3. Divide the prepared dough into 4 equal portions and roll each portion into ⅛ inches thick oval.
4. Divide the veggies, tomato, and cheese over the prepared dough ovals.
5. Fold the prepared dough ovals in half, pinch and twist the edges to seal the filling.
6. Place the calzones in the air fryer basket in batches and brush them with olive oil.
7. Air fry the calzones for 10 minutes in the preheated air fryer.
8. Serve warm.

Nutritional Facts: Calories 172; Fat 5.8g; Carbohydrate 21.5g; Protein 9.1g; Cholesterol 9mg; Sodium 304mg; Potassium 211mg

90. Vegetarian Chilli With Tofu

Prep time: 15 mins

Cooking time: 31 mins

Servings: 4

Ingredients:

- 1 tbsp. olive oil
- 1 small yellow onion, chopped
- 12 oz. extra-firm tofu, cut into small pieces
- 2 cans (14 oz.) of diced tomatoes with no salt
- 1 can (14 oz.) of kidney beans with no salt, rinsed and drained
- 1 can (14 oz.) of black beans with no salt, rinsed and drained
- 3 tbsp. chili powder
- 1 tbsp. oregano
- 1 tbsp. chopped fresh cilantro

Directions:

1. At 350°F, preheat your air fryer.
2. Spread tofu cubes in the air fryer basket and spray them with cooking spray.
3. Air fry the tofu for 10 minutes until golden brown.
4. Sauté onions with oil in a soup pot for 6 minutes.
5. Stir in oregano, chili powder, beans, and tomatoes, then cook to a boil.
6. Reduce the heat, cover, and cook on a simmer for 15 minutes.
7. Stir in tofu and mix evenly.
8. Garnish with cilantro and serve warm.

Nutritional Facts: Calories 264; Fat 10g; Carbohydrate 30.4g; Protein 17.6g; Cholesterol 0mg; Sodium 73mg; Potassium 597mg

Chapter 9: Desserts Recipes

91. Tahini Cookies

Prep time: 10 mins

Cooking time: 14 mins

Servings: 8

Ingredients:

- 1 c. unbleached white flour
- 1 c. whole wheat flour
- ⅔ c. almond meal
- ½ c. cold unsalted butter, cut into cubes
- ¾ c. sugar
- 1 tsp. vanilla extract
- Pinch of salt
- 2 tbsp. water
- ¾ c. tahini paste

Directions:

1. At 350°F, preheat your air fryer.
2. Layer two baking sheets with parchment paper.
3. Blend sugar, vanilla, salt, butter, almond meal, and flours in a food processor until crumbly.
4. Stir in tahini and water, then mix well to make a dough.
5. Knead the prepared dough, divide it into two tablespoon balls, and place them on the baking sheets.
6. Press the balls into cookies and transfer the cookies to the air fryer basket.
7. Air fry these cookies in tin batches for 14 minutes until golden brown.
8. Enjoy.

Nutritional Facts: Calories 174; Fat 7.7g; Carbohydrate 24.3g; Protein 3.3g; Cholesterol 10mg; Sodium 14mg; Potassium 61mg

92. Berry Hand Pies

Prep time: 15 mins

Cooking time: 12 mins

Servings: 8

Ingredients:

- 1 box of store-bought pie crust
- ½ C. berry jam
- ½ C. berries
- ¼ C. almond butter, melted
- 2 Tbsp. caster sugar

Directions:

1. At 375°F, preheat your air fryer.
2. Roll out the pie crusts and cut 14 (4 inches) circles out of this dough using a cookie cutter.
3. Knead the leftover dough and roll out again to cut two more circles.
4. Add two tablespoons of berry jam at the center of 8 dough circles.
5. Place the remaining dough circles on top and press the edges with a fork to seal them.
6. Brush the hand pies with almond butter and drizzle sugar on top.
7. Place the berry hand pies in the air fryer basket and air fry for 12 minutes.
8. Flip the hand pies once cooked halfway through.
9. Serve.

Nutritional Facts: Calories 167; Fat 7.3g; Carbohydrate 0g; Protein 4.3g; Cholesterol 0mg; Sodium 167mg; Potassium 637mg

93. Black Bean Brownie

Prep time: 15 mins

Cooking time: 15 mins

Servings: 8

Ingredients:

- 1 ½ c. canned (no salt) black beans, drained, rinsed
- 2 tbsp. Cocoa powder
- ½ c. quick oats
- ¼ tsp. salt
- ⅓ c. pure maple syrup
- 2 tbsp. sugar
- ¼ c. coconut oil
- 2 tsp. Pure vanilla extract
- ½ tsp. baking powder
- ½-⅔ c. chocolate chips
- Powder sugar to garnish

Directions:

1. At 350°F, preheat your air fryer.
2. Blend black beans, chocolate chips, cocoa powder, oats, salt, maple syrup, sugar, oil, vanilla, and baking powder in a blender for 2 minutes.
3. Grease an 8x8 inches pan with oil and spread the brownie dough into the pan.
4. Air fry the brownies for 15 minutes, then allow them to cool.
5. Cut the brownie into squares and garnish with powdered sugar.
6. Serve.

Nutritional Facts: Calories 260; Fat 5g; Carbohydrate 45.6g; Protein 9.7g; Cholesterol 2mg; Sodium 86mg; Potassium 700mg

94. Apple Pie Roll

Prep time: 10 mins

Cooking time: 8 mins

Servings: 4

Ingredients:

- 21 oz. Can apple pie filling
- ½ tsp. Lemon juice
- ¼ tsp. Apple pie spice
- ⅛ tsp. ground cinnamon
- 1 Tbsp. all-purpose flour
- 4 roll wrappers

Directions:

1. Mix apple pie filling with lemon juice, apple pie spice, cinnamon, and flour in a bowl.
2. Spread a roll wrapper on the working surface in a diamond shape position.
3. Add ¼ of the apple pie filling to one corner of the wrapper.
4. Fold the top and bottom of the wrapper and roll it neatly.
5. Wet the edges and press to seal the roll.
6. Place the rolls in the air fryer basket and spray with cooking spray.
7. At 400°F, preheat your air fryer.
8. Air fry the apple pie rolls for 8 minutes in the preheated air fryer.
9. Serve

Nutritional Facts: Calories 156; Fat 0.6g; Carbohydrate 34.5g; Protein 5.2g; Cholesterol 0mg; Sodium 104mg; Potassium 6mg

95. Almond Rice Pudding

Prep time: 10 mins

Cooking time: 10 mins

Servings: 6

Ingredients:

- 3 c. fat-free milk
- 1 c. white rice
- ¼ c. sugar
- 1 tsp. vanilla
- ¼ tsp. almond extract
- Cinnamon to taste
- ¼ c. toasted almonds
- Cherry compote to garnish

Directions:

1. Mix rice and milk in a medium baking dish.
2. At 350°F, preheat your air fryer.
3. Cook the pudding in the air fryer for 10 minutes.
4. Allow the pudding to cool, then stir in the rest of the ingredients.
5. Garnish with cherry compote and refrigerate for 3 hours.
6. Serve.

Nutritional Facts: Calories 220; Fat 3.4g; Carbohydrate 40.1g; Protein 7.2g; Cholesterol 6mg; Sodium 55mg; Potassium 249mg

96. Apple Hand Pies

Prep time: 15 mins

Cooking time: 10 mins

Servings: 6

Ingredients:

- 14 oz. refrigerated package pie crust (2 crusts)
- ½ (21 oz.) can of apple pie filling
- 2 tbsp. almond butter
- 3 tsp. turbinado sugar
- Caramel sauce for dipping

Directions:

1. At 350°F, preheat your air fryer.
2. Spread the pie crusts on the working surface.
3. Cut 5-inch circles out of the crusts using a cookie cutter.
4. Add two slices of apples from the pie filling at the center of each round.
5. Fold the dough circles in half and press edges with a fork to seal the filling.
6. Place the apple hand pies in the air fryer basket.
7. Brush the almond butter over the handpieces and drizzle sugar on top.
8. Cut 3 slits on top of each hand pie and air fry for 10 minutes.
9. Serve with caramel sauce.

Nutritional Facts: Calories 349; Fat 13.5g; Carbohydrate 56.3g; Protein 4.6g; Cholesterol 5mg; Sodium 17mg; Potassium 460mg

97. Air Fryer Beignets

Prep time: 10 mins

Cooking time: 12 mins

Servings: 6

Ingredients:

- 1 c. self-rising flour
- 1 c. soy yogurt
- 2 tbsp. sugar
- 1 tsp. vanilla
- 2 tbsp. melted almond butter
- ½ c. powdered sugar

Directions:

1. Mix yogurt, sugar, and vanilla in a mixing bowl.
2. Stir in flour and mix until it makes a smooth dough.
3. Knead the dough for 5 minutes, then spread into a 1inch thick rectangle.
4. Cut this dough into nine equal pieces and dust each piece with some flour.
5. Leave these dough pieces for 15 minutes.
6. At 350°F, preheat your air fryer.
7. Grease the air fryer basket with cooking oil spray.
8. Transfer the prepared dough pieces to the basket and brush them with melted butter.
9. Air fry the beignets for 12 minutes until golden brown.
10. Flip the beignets once cooked halfway through.
11. Dust the beignets with powdered sugar.
12. Serve.

Nutritional Facts: Calories 294; Fat 6.1g; Carbohydrate 52.7g; Protein 7.7g; Cholesterol 0mg; Sodium 144mg; Potassium 161mg

98. Churros

Prep time: 15 mins

Cooking time: 25 mins

Servings: 6

Ingredients:

- 1 c. water
- 4 tbsp. unsalted butter
- 2 tbsp. Packed light brown sugar
- ½ tsp. salt
- 1 c. all-purpose flour
- 2 large eggs
- 1 tsp. vanilla extract
- 3 tbsp. Granulated sugar
- ½ tsp. ground cinnamon
- Confectioner's sugar, to garnish

Directions:

1. At 350°F, preheat your air fryer.
2. Layer a rimmed baking sheet with parchment paper.
3. Mix water, butter, sugar, and salt in a saucepan and cook to a boil.
4. Remove it from the heat and allow the mixture to cool.
5. Beat in eggs, vanilla, sugar, cinnamon, and flour, then mix well until smooth.
6. Transfer the batter to the piping bag with a star-tip fitted at the end.
7. Pipe the batter into 4-6 inches churros onto the rimmed baking sheet.
8. Refrigerate them for 15 minutes to set.
9. Transfer the churros and the parchment paper to the air fryer basket in batches and air fry for 15 minutes until golden brown.
10. Garnish with confectioner's sugar.
11. Serve.

Nutritional Facts: Calories 197; Fat 9.5g; Carbohydrate 23.3g; Protein 4.3g; Cholesterol 82mg; Sodium 274mg; Potassium 51mg

99. Chocolate Souffle

Prep time: 10 mins

Cooking time: 25 mins

Servings: 8

Ingredients:

- ½ c. unsweetened cocoa powder
- 6 tbsp. hot water
- 1 tbsp. unsalted butter
- 1 tbsp. canola oil
- 3 tbsp. all-purpose flour
- 1 tbsp. Ground hazelnuts
- ¼ tsp. ground cinnamon
- 3 tbsp. dark brown sugar
- 2 tbsp. Honey
- ⅛ tsp. salt
- ¾ c. low-fat milk
- 4 egg whites
- 3 tbsp. granulated sugar
- 1 tsp. confectioners' sugar

Directions:

1. At 375°F, preheat your air fryer.
2. Grease six one-cup souffle ramekins with cooking spray.
3. Mix cocoa with hot water in a small bowl.

4. Melt butter in a heavy pan over medium heat.
5. Stir in canola oil and mix well.
6. Add cinnamon, flour, and hazelnuts, then cook for 1 minute.
7. Stir in salt, honey, and brown sugar, then remove from the heat.
8. Stir in cocoa mixture, then mix well.
9. Beat egg whites in an electric mixer on high speed until foamy.
10. Add granulated sugar, then beat until it forms stiff peaks.
11. Slowly add the egg whites to the cocoa batter, then stir until evenly mixed.
12. Divide the souffle batter into the ramekins and air fry for 15-20 minutes in the preheated air fryer.
13. Garnish with sugar and serve.

Nutritional Facts: Calories 121; Fat 4.5g; Carbohydrate 19.3g; Protein 4.1g; Cholesterol 6mg; Sodium 75mg; Potassium 150mg

100. Oatmeal Cookies

Prep time: 15 mins

Cooking time: 17 mins

Servings: 16

Ingredients:

- 1 ½ c. unbleached all-purpose flour
- 1 tsp. baking soda
- ½ tsp. salt
- ½ tsp. cinnamon
- ⅛ tsp. ground cloves
- 1 c. unsalted butter, melted
- 1 c. light brown sugar
- ½ c. granulated sugar
- 2 large eggs
- 1 tsp. pure vanilla extract
- 3 c. rolled oats
- 1 ½ c. raisins

Directions:
1. At 350°F, preheat your air fryer.
2. Mix flour with cloves, cinnamon, salt, and baking soda in a medium bowl.
3. Beat sugars with butter in a bowl of the electric mixer until smooth.
4. Stir in eggs and vanilla, then blend for 1 minute.
5. Add flour mixture and mix until smooth.
6. Fold in raisins and oats, then mix well. Cover and refrigerate for 10 minutes.
7. Drop the raisin batter onto baking sheets into 3 inches of cookies. Refrigerate them for 15 minutes.
8. Air fry the cookies in batches for 17 minutes in the preheated air fryer.
9. Allow the cookies to cool.
10. Serve warm.

Nutritional Facts: Calories 329; Fat 13.3g; Carbohydrate 50g; Protein 4.6g; Cholesterol 54mg; Sodium 250mg; Potassium 201mg

Chapter 10: 35 Day Meal Plan

Day	Breakfast	Lunch	Snacks	Dinner	Dessert
1	Egg Frittata	Spicy Sweet Potato Soup	Crispy Beans	Chicken Zucchini Skewers	Tahini Cookies
2	Ezekiel Bread Toast	Barley Carrot Soup	Hummus	Saucy Duck Breast	Berry Hand Pies
3	Buckwheat Crepes	Cream Of Mushroom Soup	Sweet Potato Crisp	Chicken Wraps	Black Bean Brownie
4	Blueberry Spelt Muffins	Carrot Ginger Soup	Cardamom Tea Cookies	Roasted Chicken	Apple Pie Roll
5	Breakfast Cookies	Sweet Potato Lentil Soup	Whole-Wheat Pretzel	Chicken Brats	Almond Rice Pudding
6	Morning Oats	Cauliflower Soup	Mini-Meatballs	Balsamic Chicken Roast	Apple Hand Pies
7	Spinach Omelet	Butternut Squash Soup	Potato Pancakes	Chicken Piccata	Air fryer Beignets
8	Breakfast Quiches	Lentil Chicken Soup	Spiced Pita Chips	Chicken Mushroom Ragu	Churros
9	Crusted French Toast	French Onion Soup	Zucchini Chips	Chicken Quesadillas	Chocolate Souffles

10	Egg Frittata	Turkey Noodle Soup	Crispy Beans	Crusted Chicken	Oatmeal Cookies
11	Ezekiel Bread Toast	Marinated Mushrooms	Hummus	Honey Dijon Chicken	Tahini Cookies
12	Buckwheat Crepes	Barley Risotto	Sweet Potato Crisp	Garlic Herb Chicken	Berry Hand Pies
13	Blueberry Spelt Muffins	Black Bean Wrap	Cardamom Tea Cookies	Crispy Air fried Chicken	Black Bean Brownie
14	Breakfast Cookies	Vegetable Kebabs	Whole-Wheat Pretzel	Sesame Chicken	Apple Pie Roll
15	Morning Oats	Buffalo Cauliflower	Mini-Meatballs	Spicy Beef Kebabs	Almond Rice Pudding
16	Spinach Omelet	Sumac Roasted Cauliflower	Crispy Beans	Pork Tenderloin With Balsamic Sauce	Apple Hand Pies
17	Breakfast Quiches	Sesame-Crusted Tofu	Hummus	Pork With Herbes De Provence	Air fryer Beignets
18	Crusted French Toast	Stuffed Eggplant	Sweet Potato Crisp	Pork Chops With Black Currant Sauce	Churros
19	Egg Frittata	Vegetable Calzone	Cardamom Tea Cookies	Pork Fajitas	Chocolate Souffles
20	Ezekiel Bread Toast	Vegetarian Chilli With Tofu	Whole-Wheat Pretzel	Spiced Pork Medallions	Oatmeal Cookies
21	Buckwheat Crepes	Sesame-Crusted Tofu	Mini-Meatballs	Curried Pork Tenderloin	Tahini Cookies
22	Blueberry Spelt Muffins	Black Bean Wrap	Potato Pancakes	Beef Stew With Fennel	Apple Pie Roll
23	Breakfast Cookies	Barley Carrot Soup	Spiced Pita Chips	Beef Brisket Stew	Almond Rice Pudding

24	Morning Oats	Vegetarian Chilli With Tofu	Zucchini Chips	Beef Barley Stew	Berry Hand Pies
25	Spinach Omelet	Air fried Swordfish	Crispy Beans	Asian Pork Tenderloin	Black Bean Brownie
26	Breakfast Quiches	Air fried Sole	Cardamom Tea Cookies	New York Strip Steak	Almond Rice Pudding
27	Crusted French Toast	Shrimp Kebabs	Whole-Wheat Pretzel	Shepherd's Pie	Apple Hand Pies
28	Ezekiel Bread Toast	Spicy Beef Kebabs	Onion Rings	Green Salad with Chickpeas	Air fryer Beignets
29	Egg Frittata	Roasted Salmon	Mini-Meatballs	Pork Tenderloin With Fennel Sauce	Churros
30	Ezekiel Bread Toast	Grilled Salmon With Maple Glaze	Potato Pancakes	Asian Pork Tenderloin	Chocolate Souffles
31	Buckwheat Crepes	Grouper With Tomato Sauce	Spiced Pita Chips	Beef Barley Stew	Almond Rice Pudding
32	Blueberry Spelt Muffins	Crusted Snapper Curry	Zucchini Chips	Chicken Wraps	Tahini Cookies
33	Breakfast Cookies	Halibut With Tomato Relish	Zucchini Chips	Shepherd's Pie	Apple Pie Roll
34	Morning Oats	Air fried Cod Pocket	Spiced Pita Chips	Chicken Wraps	Almond Rice Pudding
35	Spinach Omelet	Chipotle Spiced Shrimp	Potato Pancakes	Beef Barley Stew	Berry Hand Pies

Conclusion

Dietary Approaches to Stop Hypertension can be your next big step to improving your health. I hope the facts and the 100 low-sodium, healthy, air fryer DASH diet recipes shared in this cookbook will easily help you get started with this diet.

The first few days will be difficult, but once you understand how this diet works for you, it will get easier. Remember to check the sodium content in every product you use in your recipes. Practice the habit of reading labels and refrain from things that are loaded with sodium.

Who says salt-free, low-sodium food cannot be delicious? You just need to use the right combination of ingredients, and that is where this book can help you! Go ahead, pick your favorite recipes from my collection and give them a try.

Manufactured by Amazon.ca
Bolton, ON